Edward de Bono studied at Christ Church, Oxford (as a Rhodes Scholar). He also holds a PhD from Cambridge and an MD from the University of Malta. He has held appointments at the universities of Oxford, London, Cambridge and Harvard.

In 1967 de Bono invented the now commonly used term 'lateral thinking' and, for many thousands, indeed millions, of people worldwide, his name has since become a symbol of creativity and new thinking. He has written numerous books, which have been translated into 34 languages, and his advice is sought by Nobel laureates and world leaders alike.

ATLAS OF MANAGEMENT THINKING

Edward de Bono

Vermilion
LONDON

1 3 5 7 9 10 8 6 4 2

Vermilion, an imprint of Ebury Publishing,
20 Vauxhall Bridge Road,
London SW1V 2SA

Vermilion is part of the Penguin Random House group of companies
whose addresses can be found at global.penguinrandomhouse.com

Penguin
Random House
UK

This edition first published in the United Kingdom by Vermilion in 2017
First published by Maurice Temple Smith Ltd 1981

www.penguin.co.uk

A CIP catalogue record for this book is available from the British Library

ISBN 9781785041105

Printed and bound in Great Britain by Clays Ltd, St Ives PLC

Penguin Random House is committed to a sustainable future for
our business, our readers and our planet. This book is made from
Forest Stewardship Council® certified paper.

INTRODUCTION

This unusual book needs an introduction more than most. I want to explain its purpose and why I wrote (and drew) it.

The book has two clear purposes: right-brain thinking, and communication. This may be the first book ever to be written specifically for the right side of the brain – the intuitive side. I am not aware of any other book with that deliberate purpose. Its function as a communication system arises from that first purpose, but it can be used independently, and it was this use in communication that suggested the word 'atlas' in the title. An atlas is a visual reference system, and although thinking is an abstract subject I believe we can create perceptual maps of its use.

Many people are aware of the value and power of intuition: of those feelings and images that are part of thinking but cannot be verbalised. Over the last few years there has been a good deal of experimental work that has sought to distinguish the operations of the two halves of the human brain. It is in the left half of the brain that the speech centre is located and this half seems to control our physical activities as well. In left-handed people it is the reverse. Left-brain thinking seems to be word-based and to proceed in a logical, sequential manner. It follows that all books tend to be left-brain books. The right brain, it seems, is concerned with a different sort of thinking: with images and whole patterns and impressions and what we call intuition.

This sharp division of functions smacks a little bit of Victorian phrenology. For my part I do not really care whether these 'right-brain functions' actually take place only in the right brain or elsewhere. What I do think is important is the recognition of a type of thinking that is not dominated by language. Right-brain thinking happens to have become a useful term of reference for this. I shall also use the term 'image thinking', recognising that this spans all the way from actual images to undefined feelings.

Anyone who has been to one of my seminars knows that I accompany every thought with an image drawn on an overhead projector. In the course of a day I might cover five hundred feet of acetate with these images. They are 'idea pictures' which represent relationships, functions and happenings, not physical reality. I believe that such images can be more powerful than words for conveying ideas because, unlike words, they exist completely at one moment in time. A scientist obtains the same effect when he looks at a graph of a complex relationship that would take many seconds to describe in words.

We could describe a chair with a string of words: 'a platform about eighteen inches off the ground and supported by a leg at each corner and....' We never do this because we have a vague visual image that covers all chairs, and we only need to trigger this image with the single word 'chair'. When we taste wine we may appreciate the sensations at the front of the mouth, the top, the back and the sides. We may appreciate the bouquet and the after-taste. We do not have to verbalise it all. It is enough to sense the 'flavour'. We may form a taste image just as we form a visual image for a chair.

Unfortunately we do not have non-verbal images for complex situations. The reason is that we have never experienced such situations with any 'sense'. We have only recognised them intellectually, so there is no sense-image storage. The specific, and perhaps too bold, purpose of this book is to create a repertiore of just such non-verbal sense-images for management situations. The sense to be used is that of sight – hence the drawings. The drawings do not have to be accurate and descriptive but they do have to be simple enough to lodge in the memory. They should not be examined in detail in the way a diagram is examined, because they are not diagrams. They are intended to convey the 'flavour' of the situation described.

Such images would be used in right-brain thinking. This would help us to do right-brain thinking about situations which are otherwise restricted to left-brain attention. I see a synergy between the two sides: a continual moving backwards and forwards between verbal and non-verbal thinking.

I now come to the function of the book as a management communication system. In a sense this is its 'atlas' function. If you know someone has an atlas you can refer him to a page number and grid reference so that he can locate what you wish him to look at. The images in this book can be used in exactly the same way. You do not have to remember the images or be able to draw them. All you do is to ensure that each of your executives (and other businesses you deal with) has a copy of this book. You then treat it as you would an atlas. There are no grid references – just page numbers.

'If we are not careful I can see ourselves heading into a page 164.'

'As for Jackson, it is a typical page 99.'

'I don't like this new plan at all – see page 98.'

'We talk a lot about productivity but it is just page 16 stuff.'

'I agree there is an opportunity but that proposal is page 67.'

'Is page 182 familiar?'

The comments may be written or spoken. What are the advantages of such a system in terms of convenience?

1. It provides a shorthand that can convey very quickly the flavour of a complex situation. You do not even need the expanse of a postcard. In fact it is a much better help to communication than a laptop, which only enables people to be even more verbose.

2. Because the 'atlas' takes responsibility, it is possible to be much more blunt and direct. There is no need to say things in an oblique way and to beat about the bush. Signalling a page number is never embarassing. This can be important both in negotiations and also in appraisals of performance.

3. The Repertoire provides a convenient labelling system for some standard management situations.

4. The person sending the communication has to clarify his own thoughts in order to select the most appropriate image. This may be the most important aspect of all.

5. The system can be used in group discussions as a third party reference system.

6. It can be used as an aide memoire when a person is thinking to himself about a situation. The images act like questions: 'Is this the case here?'

For a long time I have been convinced that the business world uses more thinking than any other world. This is inevitable both because of the rate of change and also because of the need to make things happen. There are always things to be done: problems to be solved; opportunities to be discovered and developed; ventures to be conceived; projects to be organised; forecasts to be made; assessments to be assessed. The thinking is very different from that in the academic world or even the scientific world where times does not matter and coasting is easy.

As I have written on other occasions, I have been impressed by the motivation of business executives with regard to thinking. Of course there are executives who believe that seat-of-the-pants experience is enough. Of course there are those who believe that business is a matter of collecting data and sorting it. Nevertheless there are a considerable number who do believe in the importance of thinking. Many of these, in turn, believe that there is nothing that can be done to improve thinking and that their personal intelligence is quite sufficient anyway; but there are others who have just as much confidence in their thinking skills but who accept that thinking is an operating skill and like any other operating skill it can be improved through direct attention.

In routine and semi-routine operations experience probably is the best master. But running up and down a groove successfully does not get one out of the groove. There was a time when grooved thinking was enough. Sustained economic growth endorsed traditional methods that were reliable and sufficient. In a changing and competitive world more and better grooved thinking may not be enough. Innovation and creativity are important but that is not what I am writing about here. What I am referring to is a broad range of operating thinking skills: in short all the thinking we have to do if the groove can no longer do our thinking for us. In particular we need a great deal of conceptual thinking, for in the end the success or failure of a business rests on its concepts. A concept may only take a few seconds to design but the lack of a good one can mean the failure of a billion dollar corporation. It is the more successful organisations that sense the need to develop further thinking skills because they attribute their success to their thinking. The less successful ones see no need because they blame their failure on circumstances.

A few years ago I coined the term 'operacy', which is the skill of getting things done, of making things happen. I believe that, in education, operacy should be treated on an equal basis with literacy and numeracy. Traditional education is much too concerned with descriptive thinking because there is an odd notion that from a full information field the right action automatically emerges.

To my mind the most dangerous fallacy in education is the belief that intelligence and thinking skill are the same thing. It is dangerous in two ways: firstly because it follows that the intelligent need no training in thinking and secondly because such training would be pointless for the less intelligent. Unfortunately highly intelligent people are not always effective thinkers. So much so that in our work in the Cognitive Research Trust in Cambridge we have coined the term 'intelligence trap' to describe thinking habits which may actually put the intelligent youngster at a disadvantage. For example, the person who can articulate and argue well can seem to justify any perception, and as a result his thinking effort is directed towards this argumentation rather than to the (more important) perceptual exploration. There is a growing awareness that even the intelligent need to pay direct attention to thinking skills.

Once we decide to pay direct attention to our thinking skills – instead of regarding them as an automatic part of our intelligence – there are many things that can be done. There are techniques both in lateral thinking and in basic thinking skills that can be practised and used. Software for the mind is no less valuable than software for computers. Mathematics, itself, is a software system.

This book can now be seen against the background of what I have written above, as an attempt to create a visual meta-language for situations. I believe it to be worth doing. The more we enrich our perception the more powerful it becomes. As computers take over more and more of our thinking, perception will always remain the most important part. The clarity with which we see a situation is the basis for any subsequent decision or action. That clarity is not built up piecemeal but obtained through a flash of recognition. We do not measure the length of a friend's nose in order to recognise his face. It is this type of recognition that the book aims to help. Sometimes we call it intuition.

PAGE INDEX

CONFRONTATION

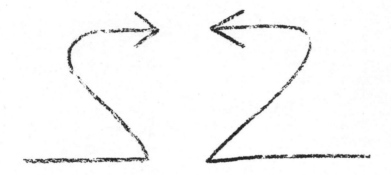

1   CLASH, CONFRONTATION, ARGUMENT OR...

If the two rearing arrows look like cobras poised to strike each other, the resemblance is intended. They seem to draw back in an arch only to get more vigour into the attack. There might also be a suggestion of a pause in the confrontation as each side enjoys the tensing of the muscles that precedes an actual clash. I have written at length elsewhere of the peculiarity and wastefulness of the Western habit of argument and clash. I blame it on medieval theologians who developed the system in order to confront and annihilate heresies that challenged the integrity of the Church. In turn they adopted the habit from those Greek philosophers who believed that dialectic was a useful mental exercise. Much later the method of dialectic clash was polished up by Hegel and adopted by Marx. Eastern cultures certainly know about the clash principle – the yin and yang of the

Chinese and the Japanese Sumo wrestlers – but it is not used as a method of getting change or making decisions. What matters most is that we should accept the peculiarity of the method rather than assume it is the natural and only way to behave.

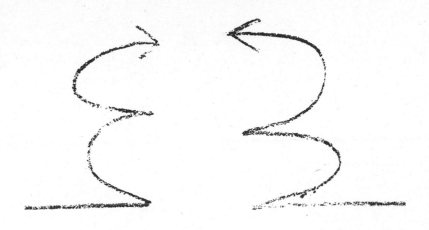

2 A SORT OF RITUAL DANCE

The suggestion here is of several steps in a ritual dance of confrontation. As in most dances there is advance and apparent retreat, only to take up a fresh position for the next advance. We can be locked into the ritual just as we become locked into a dance sequence once we have entered upon it. Failure to take the right step at the right time leads to deception or inadequacy. The steps no longer have a logical reference to the purpose of the dance. The reference is merely to the integrity of the dance as an end in itself. In a way, failure to come through with the right steps is deception, because most social interaction is based on expectations of behaviour and to set up expectations and then thwart them must qualify as deception. The main point is that the clash procedure becomes an end in itself. The outcome or the purpose is secondary. Once it becomes an end in itself then it becomes worth doing and it becomes a profession in itself just as being a dancer is a profession. Our current systems of adversary law and politics are examples of such professionalism. So are trade union negotiations. The logic of the situation demands intelligent behaviour but the logic is that of the dance itself and does not necessarily serve the original purpose of the dance.

3 TRUMPING WITH A FACT

The relationship between facts, perceptions and values is an extremely complex one. In an argument, whoever can produce the unexpected fact has a temporary advantage, as suggested in the drawing. It might therefore be imagined that a parade of relevant facts would by itself solve any argument. If that were so then computers could well do our arguing for us. Unfortunately, interpretation of the facts and the integration of the facts into the argument are matters for perception, which links the facts to our value system and our experience. The purpose of an argument is never to be objective. It is to be subjective about an objective situation. Since any argument that is not purely academic is about how the future is to happen then there is much room for subjectivity, both about how we think the future will happen and about how we should like it to happen. The practical point, of course, is never to parade all the facts at the beginning but to use them as a military commander might unleash the cavalry squadrons he has kept hidden below the brow of the hill. Arguments are not about facts but about the tactical display of facts.

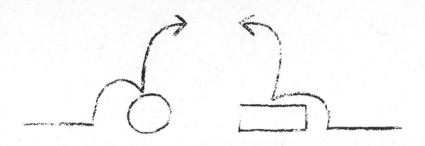

4 DIFFERENT VALUES

It could be said that in Western society religion has performed a considerable disservice by providing a more or less uniform system of social values – the Christian ethic. Since this value system is so pervasive and so accepted there has never really been a need to develop other value systems that arise from actual social situations. The Marxist value system arose in this vacuum of values and it arose from the multiplying effect that machinery had on man's labour. Once Marxism was a value system then capitalism and free enterprise tried to coalesce as a value system – largely unsuccessfully. We desperately need to develop new situational value systems, otherwise we are tied to lumbering dogma or immediate gain or defensivesness. So what are the different value bases in a particular argument? Are values more than strategic guidelines? Are they more than a series of taboos? With a taboo a person cannot allow himself to see himself doing or saying something – it is an infringement of his image. No one can ever be explicit about his own value system because he is inside it. Any request for such explicitness is met by vague waffle and stereotyped pantomime response. It is for the other party to examine the values of the opponent.

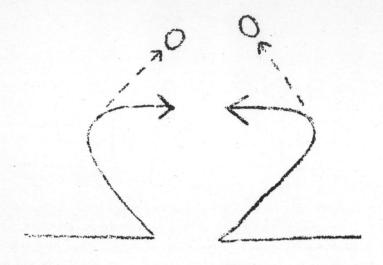

5 DIFFERENT OBJECTIVES

It is much too easy to take for granted that both sides in an argument have the same over-all objective and are engaged in argument as to how that objective can be reached. Conversely when two sides start out with widely different overt objectives it may be easy to overlook such common objectives as may be present. It is easy to assume that both workers and management in a plant have as a common objective the survival of that plant. In practice once one side thinks that the opposing party holds this objective firmly then the other feels no need to hold it as well. A different objective can be chosen: for example a rise in the wages of skilled workers at the expense of the less skilled who will be laid off by management as it pursues the objective of survival. The avoidance of blackmail may become so over-riding an objective that it obscures all other logic. Would there be much point in clarifying the objectives of those involved in an argument? Probably not, for tactical shifts at any moment may run counter to them. As with values, it is probably best to assess your opponent's objectives rather than to ask him for them.

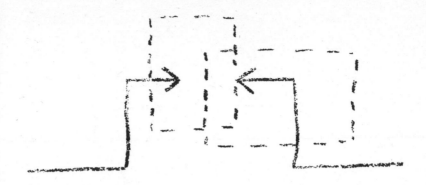

6 DIFFERENT PERCEPTIONS

For some years I have been running what is the largest programme in the world for the direct teaching of thinking as a curriculum subject in schools. There are several million children involved and some countries have adopted the programme for all their schools. The programme is largely to do with the perceptual side of thinking. Culturally and in education we have neglected this side. We have developed superb processing systems for thinking: as in mathematics and computer sorting. Yet processing is only a small part of thinking. Logical processing can do no more than service the perceptions we start out with. The skills of salesmanship and political demagogy are virtually the only methods we have for changing perception. Even if the two sides in an argument have the same value system and the same objective there can still be a fierce argument because the perceptions of the same situation are different. Perception is the most tricky and the most fascinating aspect of the mind. The brain acts as a superb pattern-making system which allows experience to organise itself into patterns. Once the patterns are formed they direct attention and organise the perception of the present. A designer looks at a table in a manner different from a housewife or a furniture manufacturer. Sometimes there are the most startling surprises when we come to realise how someone else is looking at a situation which, to us, could only be perceived in one way.

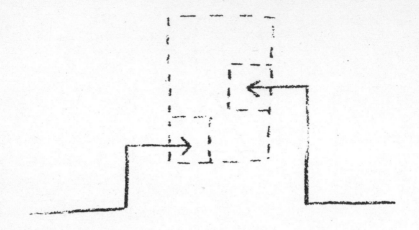

7 BOTH SIDES ARE RIGHT

There is a story about the man who painted half his car black and the other half white so that if he was involved in an accident he could enjoy hearing the witnesses contradict each other. The most common source of any argument is that both sides are absolutely right but each is looking at a different part of the situation. The parts that are being looked at may be very different but there is a uniformity about the emotion generated. The wife likes the car because it is easy to drive and to park. The husband does not like the car because it does not reflect his status. The emotions of like and dislike are just as broad as if they had arisen from a total survey of the car. In practice it is extraordinarily difficult to tear ourselves away from that tiny part of the situation which has attracted our attention and aroused our emotions, in order to consider the whole. Once perception has triggered emotion then emotion leads perception. In most cases awareness (of values, objectives, perceptions) is a great help. In this case it is not. You may well know that the other person's reaction is based on a tiny part of the situation but there is not much you or he can do about it. Except perhaps to split the argument into two.

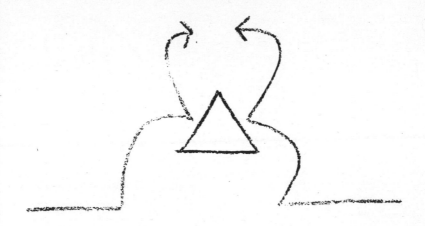

8 ARGUING ABOUT A MATTER OF PRINCIPLE

Most serious arguments are based on matters of principle. Most trivial arguments are said to be based on matters of principle. Why should principles matter so much? Why cannot we be more pragmatic about our moment to moment behaviour? The answer probably lies in the way so called principles set up expectations for the future. When we claim to be arguing about principle we are often arguing about the 'ratchet effect'. When a point is conceded at one time then that becomes the baseline for future expectations. The other reason we claim so often to be arguing about a matter of principle is that there is so little substance in many arguments that a reference to principle is necessary in order to sustain the argument. It is always possible to fashion a principle to fit the argument of the moment. We become trapped by our dexterity in doing so. Anyone with any pretensions to debating skill should be able to fashion an important principle to sustain any weak argument. Principles are like the moon that can be reflected in a thousand pools – if we choose to look in the right direction into a pool.

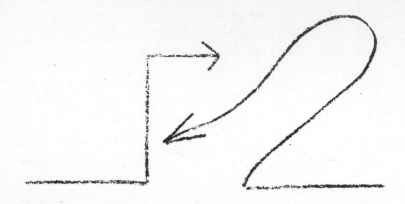

9 DESTRUCTIVE ARGUMENTS

I am not sure which is the more enjoyable: to win an argument or to annihilate the opponent. Instead of building a case for ourselves we attack the opponent or his case. Attack is rather easy. We choose our frame of reference and attack something for not fitting it. We can attack an orange for not being an apple. No matter what is being done we attack it for not being enough. No matter how worthwhile a project seems we attack it for the hidden and sinister purposes behind it. If something is done that benefits a particular group then that group is being bribed or bought off. If something is couched in general terms then it is too vague and ill-defined. If something is popular then people are being conned. If something is unpopular then it is being forced on people. If something stops early then there is lack of persistence. If something is carried on then it is flogging a dead horse or blind ambition. The most curious thing is that we actually esteem this sort of thinking and consider it clever instead of facile.

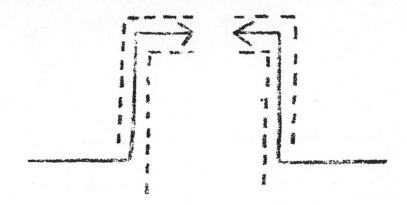

10 DOCTRINAIRE ARGUMENT

Like accoutred knights charging towards each other in a formal tournament, an argument carried out within the formal confines of opposing doctrines becomes simple power play. The words, thoughts and concepts uttered are part of the decor. They are not meant to be listened to. They are just ways of filling time whilst the realities of power assert themselves. There are rare occasions when a skilled contestant can turn the rigidity of a doctrine against the proponent of that doctrine – like the devil quoting scripture. That might work with the *philosophe* who put together the doctrine in the first place but it is unlikely to work with a follower who is able to live with all sorts of inconsistencies so long as a few slogans can be repeated again and again. One would think that the more rigid a doctrine the more brittle it should be. There is therefore this temptation to argue against doctrine. But doctrine exists in the belief system and can therefore be replaced or atrophied but not attacked.

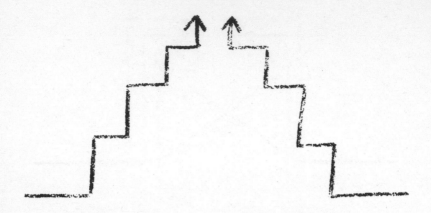

11 CONSTRUCTIVE ARGUMENT

If we must have argument then perhaps it could be constructive. Instead of regarding all confrontation situations as zero-sum games (in which for one side to win the other must lose) we could attempt to extract gains for both sides. The direction of the arrows in the drawing suggests an upward movement. Instead of facing each other in a clash the arrows are aligned in their upward movement. They also approach closer and closer. Stage by stage a constructive outcome is being built. At each stage there is an apparent confrontation which is quickly turned into a constructive step. One of the most important things about constructive arguments is that they almost have to be step by step. It is unrealistic to expect one side or other to put forward a constructive proposal that is immediately acceptable to the other side. Step by step progress is more practical. At each step both sides must see a gain.

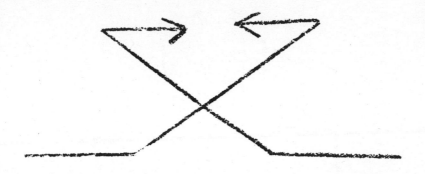

12 CROSS-PURPOSES

I was very tired after the long flight from London to Sydney and on the television show someone attacked what I had just been saying. My normal reaction would have been to attack back but I was too tired, so I said: 'If I understood from what I have been saying what you obviously understand – then I would agree with you.' A large number of arguments are at cross-purposes because one or other (or both) sides is interpreting incorrectly the position of the other side. It is a useful exercise to put – and answer – the obvious question: 'What are we arguing about?' This is one of the cases in which the need to express something in definite terms can deflate the argument. It often emerges from the answer to such a question that there really is no argument. There is no real point of disagreement or conflict. 'We are agreed on these points – I do not know what we have been arguing about.'

PRODUCTIVITY

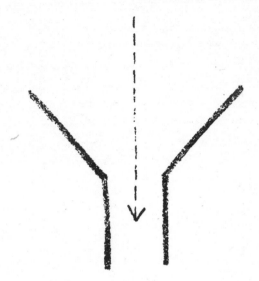

13 EFFICIENCY

As a concept 'efficiency' seems simple enough. It must mean achieving the highest output with the minimum effort. There is attached to it an element of ratio between input and output. As a concept it is highly usable. Having acknowledged its usefulness, it might be as well to look at some of the problems. If the output seems to be fixed (for example a particular product or a particular market) then efficiency means reducing the cost of that output. This starts out as sensible cost-saving and value-engineering but imperceptibly the boundary is crossed and we enter the realm of skimping. So Western automobile makers put as few extras into their cars as possible – the Japanese put as many as possible. You can cut down on cost per unit by continuing with the old machinery. There is another problem. Efficiency may mean the best use of resources at this moment in time. Something which is seen to be efficient at the moment may not be efficient if the future is taken into consideration – and the other way round. There is also the element of choice. If we choose to use our resources in the most efficient place at the moment we may avoid those areas which are not so efficient but which will be more valuable in the future. Then there is the problem of maximum efficiency. If everything is working at its optimum level with no spare fat then it is all rather brittle because there are no cushions to absorb changes and downturns. It is a dilemma: if we strive to be ever more efficient for this moment in time, does that make us more efficient for the future?

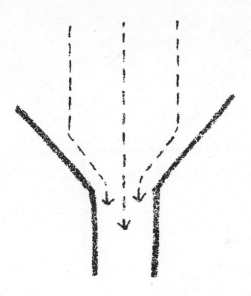

14 EFFECTIVENESS

The concept of effectiveness is different from the concept of efficiency. As is suggested in the drawing, it does not eschew waste. The concept of effectiveness means that a decision is made to do something and to do it effectively. Then all resources are applied to this task – even if it means an excess of effort as judged by efficiency. Instead of allocating resources in the most efficient way there is a list of priorities. Starting at the top, resources are used effectively on each in turn. If resources run out before the end is reached then the list stops there. In practice effectiveness must imply a degree of efficiency. What is important is that the starting point is so different. Instead of there constantly being the efficiency 'ratio' in mind there is the decision to do something effectively. In practice this means that attention tends to be more on the output than on the input. 'What is the result of our efforts?' rather than 'What is the least cost of our efforts?'

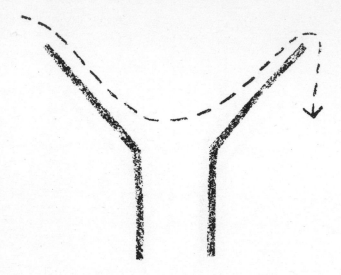

15 WASTE

The drawing suggests an obvious example of waste. The arrow has missed the intended direction completely. In this case the structure of the funnel that was supposed to channel effort in the right direction has failed to do so. Without structure it is difficult to keep effort aimed in the right direction. Structures may be physical as with machinery. Structures may be organisational in terms of who commands who and who reports to whom. Structures may be mental in terms of team spirit or political aims. Should we set up structures so that ordinary behaviour becomes highly effective or would we set up structures that demand special behaviour? Do we chase the free range hens and find the eggs as best we can or do we put the hens into a battery?

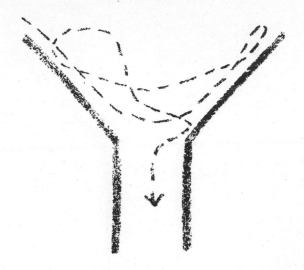

16 FLURRY

A great deal of effort and sloshing about is suggested by the drawing. There is no lack of energy. Nor is there any manifest waste. But compared to the drawings of efficiency and effectiveness there does seem to be a lot of frantic unnecessary activity. On the whole energy does not direct itself. Unguided enthusiasm is not the same as effectiveness. Motivation may not be enough by itself. I know of one company where everyone became so highly motivated that most of them left, because they now found frustrating a pace which they had found acceptable before. Activity is not the same as effectiveness. The skilled sportsman seems to have more time and to do things more slowly than the less skilled one. Hyperactive children have no shortage of energy but great difficulty in focusing that energy on achieving some defined task.

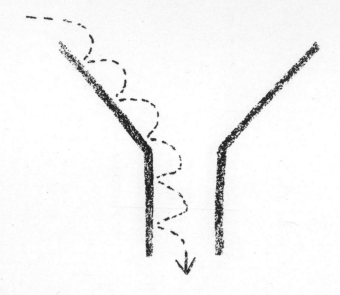

17 DETAIL

There are some people who live in a world of detail. There are others who can see only the broad view and the general thrust of an operation. The drawing suggests the painstaking, detailed approach – but carried too far. At every step there is a return to the security of the guiding walls to check if everything is still alright. There is an excess of procedure. The main thrust of the operation has not been internalised or understood. Instead of a person looking across the room to the door there is a groping in the dark so that a painstaking progress is made towards the door through constant reference to each piece of furniture. In a way this is the essence of bureaucracy. Instead of the bureaucracy continuing to serve the main purpose for which it has been set up there is an obsession with procedure, because procedure has to serve as the guideline in the absence of anything else. There is no obvious waste, there is no flurry either – but everything is very slow.

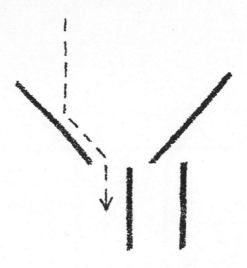

18 STRUCTURAL FAULT

The two parts of the funnel are not aligned. So obvious a structural fault must be easy to diagnose and put right. In practice, however, it often happens that the operating thrust of different parts of the organisation are not aligned since the structure has evolved with reference to one part rather than the whole. In the drawing some of the input to the funnel will follow the right direction. That type of structural error is rather more difficult to diagnose than the type where the results are always bad. A structure that is sometimes effective and sometimes ineffective suggests that there is nothing wrong with the structure itself – merely with the people operating it: sometimes they are inclined to become slack. In such cases judgement by results may not be enough. There is need for a structural overview. In turn this cannot be obtained through asking each part of the organisation for its views. Each part may actually be quite in order. It is only the overall alignment of the parts that is at fault.

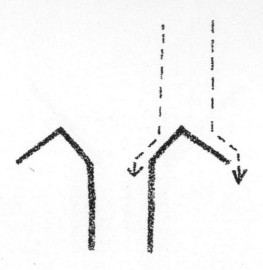

19 NO FLEXIBILITY

The peculiar design of funnel shown in the drawing would work perfectly well so long as the input was pretty focused. If this were to be the case then no deficiency at all would be noticed in the behaviour of the funnel. So an organisation may work very well if its people are motivated or skilled but suddenly run into bad trouble if the level of motivation or skill should fall. The catchment area shown for the funnel is very small. In engineering terms the tolerance is small. To be truly effective a system needs to be designed to cope with a wide range of inputs. It should be flexible: not in terms of changing to meet the inputs but in terms of being broad enough to channel different inputs in the required direction. It is easy enough to design systems that work well when everything is going well. After all, we design for success. What is more important is to design structures that can cope well with different inputs.

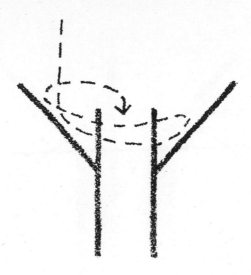

20 DIFFICULT

How easy should things be? How much effort should be required to make something work? The funnel structure shown in the drawing is certainly usable but it is much more difficult to use than the ordinary funnel shown in the drawing for 'efficiency'. How do we know how difficult something is? If we look only at the output we may not learn anything, because if everyone is putting in the right amount of effort the system may still work in the same way as the arrow in the drawing does eventually find its way in the right direction. If things are too easy might not people become lazy and fall asleep? Might they fail to get satisfaction from what they are doing? These are important questions but I doubt whether anyone would deliberately design difficulty into a task (they would probably choose variety). The more important question is whether we know – or have any way of finding out – whether the structure is making things more difficult than they need be.

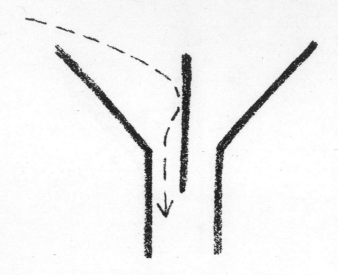

21 STRUCTURAL IMPROVEMENT

Given the idiom of these drawings the change shown in the drawing is probably an improvement. It would not make any difference if fluid was being poured into the funnel, but if the arrow traced the path of a ball-bearing dropped into the funnel then the baffle plate would speed up the descent of the ball into the tube part of the funnel. In the same way structural changes need to take account of what is to pass through the structure. Designing elegant systems in the abstract is not much use. Palaces are designed by architects to be looked at rather than lived in. Similarly some structures are designed to be discussed by management consultants rather than to make life easier for those who have to use the system. The joys of design often mean that there is a tendency to design and attempt to instal a totally new system if the old one is seen not to be working particularly well. Total design is much more satisfying than tinkering. And yet a small adjustment at the right place can make a significant difference. Also implied in the drawing is the notion that even the adequate can be improved upon.

22 DIVERSION

The old structure is still working well but now something is diverting some of the energy and effort. When we set out to do something new we often assume that the baseline will continue as it always has done. (When we jump off the ground we do not really believe that our jump will affect the ground.) Yet it must be obvious that a structural change that channels effort in a new direction may lessen the flow of effort in the old direction. The paradox of diversion is that whenever we want to divert something it proves very hard to do so; but when we do not want to create a diversion we very often end up by diverting more than we wanted. Predicting the effect of a diversion is as difficult as predicting anything else that involves human choice. Trying something out is the only real test-bed. Otherwise fear of diversion will inhibit any change no matter how necessary it may be. In addition to the deliberate diversions there are the unnoticed diversions which insidiously come about and channel off effort and purpose.

DECISION

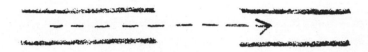

23 YES DECISION

Permission is granted. The action flows on. The switch is closed. Any decision is designed to be met with a 'yes' or agreement. If it fails to achieve that then the decision has not been properly designed. What is to be agreed or accepted is already known. The action steps are already constructed. All that is required is the 'go' signal. We talk about decisions as if there was always a point in time before which the decision was not made and after which it has been made. In practice this type of decision only occurs when someone else presents something that needs a decision. The better the preparation of that decision the closer will the result approximate to the 'go' or 'no-go' idiom. When we present ourselves with the decision we are much more inclined to drift in a certain direction leaving ourselves the option of getting out if we find we do not like it. Alternatively we accept a direction but take no action in that direction until we are sufficiently tempted to do so. The main point is that all decisions should be designed to require only a 'yes' and to elicit that 'yes'.

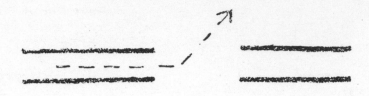

24 NO DECISION

Books that set out to give advice to management never fail to point out that a 'no' decision is not at all the same thing as failure to make a decision. This point is illustrated quite definitely in the drawing. The making of a 'no' decision is a definite action and a definite direction. It is the clear and deliberate avoidance of the direction implied by the 'yes' decision. We can hold off making a decision if we do not have enough information. The making of a 'no' decision is a positive rejection based – hopefully – on as much information as might be required for a 'yes' decision. In practice this is just hopeful because many 'no' decisions are made simply because there is need to make a decision (regarding investment for example) and insufficient information on which to base a 'yes' decision. So making a 'no' decision is a positive act of playing safe. It is rather like a child rejecting food he has not tasted because he does not have enough information to make it seem attractive.

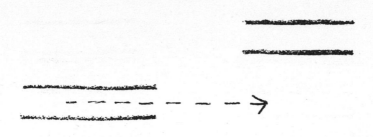

25 THE EFFORTLESS NO

It is always easier to say 'no' than to say 'yes'. This is especially the case when the action that is proposed requires some change from the usual flow of action. The drawing suggests that the 'yes' decision might require some effort. In this case the 'no' decision is not a positive rejection of the proposal but an inadequacy of temptation which might also be regarded as a lack of enterprise. 'Why should we be bothered?' is a perfectly rational response and one that is not easy to change. Suggestions of future disaster are never as convincing to the listener as they are to the talker. In practice it is difficult to distinguish the effortless 'no' from inertia, apathy, complacency and timidity. Yet – to be fair– there is no obligation on anyone to be tempted by matters which he or she does not find tempting.

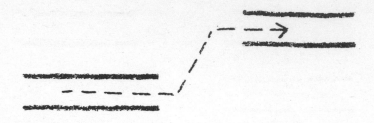

26 THE YES EFFORT

In each of the drawings up to this point no particular effort has been required of the decision maker (except, perhaps, in the positive 'no' decision). The 'yes' decision suggested in the drawing here requires a deviation from the natural flow of action. It requires effort. What should prime that effort: enthusiasm, curiosity, eagerness to change, fashion or the careful design of the proposal? Anyone who is offering a proposal that requires a 'yes' effort should be clear as to why he expects that effort to be made. The motivation of the person required to make the decision is likely to be totally different from that of the person offering the decision – yet too often the presenter of the decision imagines it to be the same. On the other hand we are fortunate indeed if we happen to be in a business that is so secure that it is enough for us to make effortless decisions that never require us to do more than flow along with established patterns.

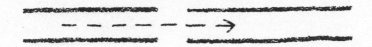

27 AN EASY DECISION

The size of a decision is always proportional to the inadequacy of the reason for making it. If information could flow directly into action there would be no need for a human decision-maker. Such a situation does often arise, for example in the feedback control of a chemical process. The sensors pick up the change which is then fed back directly to alter the temperature or some other variable. There is no need for a human decision to intervene. Some business decisions can be carried out in the same way. An investor who gives his broker an order to sell when a stock falls to a certain figure is setting up just such a system. In the drawing, the gap between the two action channels symbolises that part which has to be supplied by human intervention. This can take the form of assessing the situation or bringing into consideration other factors (political climate, human values, competitors' stance) which cannot easily be quantified.

28 A DIFFICULT DECISION

The gap between the two channels in the drawing suggests that the decision is difficult. There is a lot of work that has to be done by the decider in order to bridge the gap. Should anyone ever make difficult decisions or should he work on them – using time as an ally if necessary – until they become easy enough to be made? The question does not arise if the decision is forced by circumstances. Where it is not forced there could be a competitive advantage in making a decision that is so difficult that other people would not be prepared to make it. For example a decision by the US motor manufacturers to switch to small cars ahead of market demand would have been very difficult. For the Japanese no such decision was necessary because their home market had always been used to small cars. A decision that is easy for one group may be hard for another – not just because of different circumstances but because of different motivations. Paradoxically difficult decisions are more difficult to make in difficult times. There is less confidence and less margin for error.

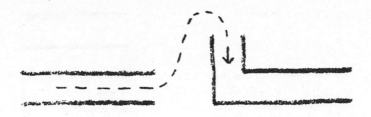

29 A DECISION THAT IS NOT OBVIOUS

In the type of decision considered so far it has been assumed that the decision is presented in a clear form. There is a request for action to produce a decision. In the drawing shown here the decision is less obvious. Having made the decision to make a decision the decider has to figure out how to make it. In a way this is a decision to present oneself with a problem and then to set about solving that problem. In the instance illustrated here the type of action required is known and what is required is to find a way of entering upon that action. This 'entry problem' is too often neglected. We tend to look only at the beginning and end of a decision. Yet the moment-to-moment implementation – the method of making the decision – may be just as important as the decision itself. Politicians know full well that a good decision badly made can be disastrous. On the other hand there are many decisions that are never made because the decider cannot figure out how to implement the decision at the very first stage. For example there are supposed to be many wives who would have left their husbands long ago if they had been able to work out how to tell him they were going.

30 A WEAK DECISION

There is no law that says that life must be difficult. There is no law that says the harder choice is the better one. In the drawing used here the effortless decision has been chosen in preference to the one that required a little more effort. The easy way out has been taken. There is no reason why this track should be any worse than the 'effort' track except that I have chosen to block off the easy track and so turn it into a dead end. This is designer's licence. I have also included a flicker in the path of the arrow to suggest that the harder choice was actually contemplated for a while. What it amounts to is that the weak choice is just as valid as the hard choice provided the tracks are examined on their merits, not in terms of weakness or laziness. The simple test question is: 'If this was an easy thing to do would I choose to do it?' If that question is applied to the hard track and gets a positive answer then it is no longer enough to go for the easy choice.

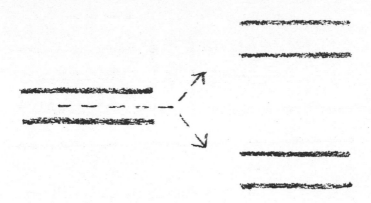

31 DECISION FOR CHOICE

A decision is not really the same as a choice although the two are very often confused. With a choice we work perceptually on the alternatives to see if we can make one so attractive that it attracts us to ignore the others; or we try to make the alternatives so unattractive that we can dismiss them one by one. A decision is more a matter of yes and no: is this thing worth doing or is it not worth doing? Clearly we could apply the same process to each of the alternatives. But we could find that all of them were worth doing and then we would have to consider comparative advantages. That is, and should be, treated differently from decision-making. Everyone knows the story of the ass which was said to have starved to death between two exactly equal bundles of hay because it could not decide (choose) which one to approach. The true moral has escaped most philosophers who use the story. The true moral seems to be that a choice is difficult not because we cannot decide which is the better but because we cannot bear to give up the one that has not been chosen.

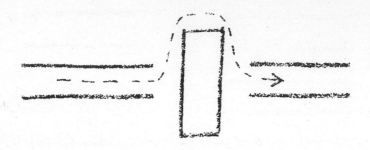

32 COPING WITH AN OBSTACLE

Obstacles are relatively easy to cope with because they are defined and tangible. They can be analysed and examined. They can be removed, or a way can be found around them. It is characteristic of decision-making that obstacles always tend to seem more real than they actually turn out to be. This is because they are used subconsciously by our emotions to shape our decisions. In Freud's idiom, the obstacles are the concretisation of subconscious urges that we cannot – or dare not – express. We cannot do much about it since the obstacles are as real to us as are ghosts to those who see them. When the decision is made and implemented the foreseen obstacles tend to evaporate. At the same time unforeseen obstacles might appear. Should obstacles be taken into account in the decision process? Probably not. The decision should be made in the first instance as if it were easy to be made. Then the obstacles are examined. Should they turn out to be insurmountable then the decision is classified as 'a good decision which cannot be carried through'. In this sense decision-making differs from problem-solving where implementation is part of the problem from the beginning.

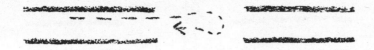

33 REFUSAL TO MAKE A DECISION

It is probably true that many decisions go away if you refuse to make them. Circumstances change and what was once a possible decision is no longer on offer. Not making a decision is really making a decision to do nothing – but it never feels like that. Making a decision makes you responsible for what happens afterwards. Not making a decision leaves fate responsible for what happens. Part of the unwillingness to make a decision is the unwillingness to turn down something – what is not chosen. Part is the unwillingness to give up the pleasure of multiple potential: being free to choose everything because you have not yet chosen anything. Part is the bother and hassle that follows the making of any decision. In matters involving people there are hurts, disappointments and outrage, all of which inhibit decision-making. Yet some people enjoy making decisions almost as an end in itself.

34 INDECISIVENESS

Is indecisiveness a mild case of refusal to make decisions, or is it something different? For some years there has been a tendency in professional examinations to use fixed multiple-choice questions. The candidate looks down the offered answers and circles A or B or C or whichever answer he thinks appropriate. Some candidates do not hesitate: they choose one answer and circle it. The more imaginative candidates see good reasons why each of the answers might just possibly be right. They waste time deciding between these alternatives and in the end do less well than their less imaginative colleagues. The brighter children or youngsters tend to do somewhat worse on such exams. So is indecisiveness an excess of imagination which can see so many possibilities in each alternative that none of them can be rejected? A more probable explanation is a lack of well defined priorities. Without priorities we look at the attractiveness of an alternative in itself: with priorities we look at its attractiveness to us.

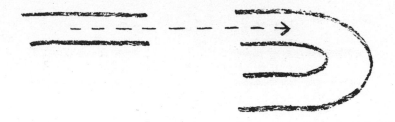

35 A COUNTER-PRODUCTIVE DECISION

Catch-22 states that in order to achieve something it may be necessary to do something that prevents that achievement. The drawing suggests that an apparently normal decision eventually returns the decider to his starting point. That a decision may turn out to have this ultimate effect can hardly be blamed on the decider, who is unable to see that far ahead. That a decision can be suspected to be counterproductive is a cause for attention. Certain decisions may thwart the very purpose for which the decision is being made. For example there may be a decision to set up an expensive data-processing facility in order to cut the costs of data-processing. There may be a decision to break off negotiations precisely in order to achieve some end in those negotiations. There may be an attempt to increase profits by so lowering the price that no profits are possible. Strange as this type of decision may seem, it is quite frequently made. The explanation is that the flavour of the decision seems right even if the substance belies the flavour.

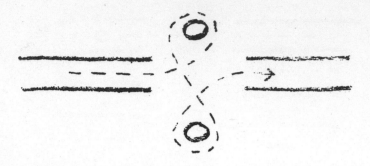

36 CONSULTATION FOR A DECISION

Ask for advice and share the risk and the blame. Most people who ask for advice about a decision are really seeking condemnation: that is to say, condemnation of the choice they do not want to make but have not the courage to reject. Advice can take the form of information, experience, perspective or perception: all of which enlarge or change the decision view. In practice the best reason for asking advice is to enlist the interest of those who might eventually be responsible for implementing the decision. If they are made to seem part of the decision they are more likely to accept it. The danger is that to give their advice some reality they suggest minor changes which have then to be included. This can be avoided by asking only for condemnations of the path that is not to be taken. That way the actual decision remains unaltered.

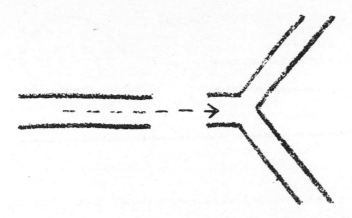

37 DILEMMA

The drawing seems to violate its own idiom. There is a decision gap and then there is a fork. Since there must presumably be a decision to take either fork there should be further decision gaps. The distortion is deliberate. I want to indicate that the decision to get involved in a dilemma is the real decision. The actual choice of routes through the dilemma is irrelevant and could just as well be decided by the toss of a coin. Once we are entrapped in a dilemma then action of one sort or another is predetermined. The only way out of a dilemma is not to get into one. In a true dilemma there probably is not much point in agonising over which route to take. The more useful decision and design stage will come after the route has been taken and the consequences faced. The secondary decisions that follow become, in fact, the primary decisions. If you must get into a dilemma then charge further into it in an attempt to gain control of your destiny once again. If there really is no choice then there is no decision to be made, so it is only a waste of time to pretend that there is.

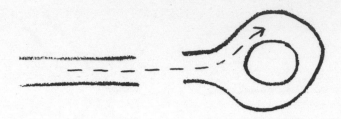

38 A POLITICAL DECISION

Functionally the political decision shown in the drawing may seem very similar to the refusal to make a decision. In both cases the decider ends up where he started from. In the case of the political decision, however, a decision is seen to be made. There is action and there is commitment. That it all leads to nothing is not so important. One purpose of a decision is to satisfy the expectations of those eager for a decision. A political decision does that as well as any other. A political decision is real enough but it is designed to leave things in the end exactly as they were in the beginning. It is not a charade, nor is it cosmetic. It is simply designed to have an effect on those watching. To do nothing in an active and important manner is a rare skill.

GETTING THERE

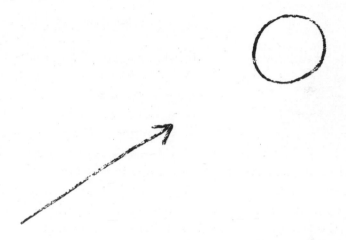

39 ON TARGET

What do we need targets for? For a sense of direction. There are some targets which we never expect to achieve but as we move towards them they give us a sense of direction. When we move 'north' we do not expect, or want, to get to the North Pole. In a similar manner, cost-cutting exercises move always in the direction of cutting costs without a specific target. We also use targets to give us a sense of achievement. A certain sales quota has been achieved and IBM honours in a special way the salesmen who have achieved one hundred per cent of quota. Targets are also used for feedback purposes. They provide a reference point and by comparing our behaviour with the reference point we can tell what adjustments are required. Target-setting is a skilled business. The simple way is that used by Gosplan, the Russian planning agency. A percentage is added to present production and that becomes the target for the five-year plan. If it is not achieved someone is to blame. If targets are too simple they merely reflect current behaviour. If they are too hard they provide no motivation. If they are just possible they provide stress.

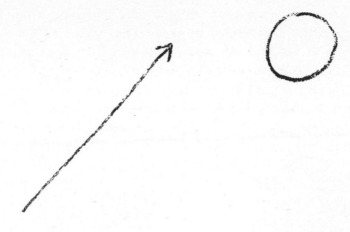

40 POOR AIM

In game shooting, some people consistently shoot badly because they always shoot at where the bird has been rather than where it has got to. Consistent poor aim often has a reason. Perhaps the target has been badly chosen or perhaps it is not clearly seen. Perhaps it is not visible at every moment. Within an organisation these are matters of communication. Who knows about the target? Is it only senior management at planning meetings or is it everyone involved in achieving it? Do the workers see the target or just hear exhortation? Perhaps the equipment is inadequate to reach the target: for example salesmen may need sales training for the new product line. At what precise point does the aim go wrong? In target practice a marksman examines carefully the cluster of shots. Is there a constant bias, or are the errors random? Poor aim is not just a failure to aim properly. It is a failure of the system and for that there may be explanations if they are sought out. Castigation and exhortation are not the best ways of doing that seeking.

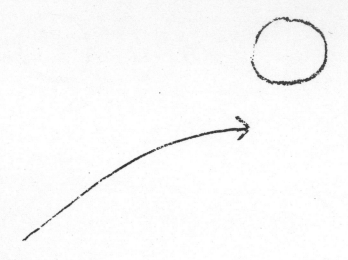

41 SHORT-FALL

The aim starts off on target but then performance falls off and the target is missed. The suggestion is that the error is not in the aim but in the energy required. It may be motivation that proves inadequate or it may be investment. A heavily advertised new launch can run out of steam when the level of advertising declines. What has been designed to sustain the effort? The situation is quite different from that of poor aim – and much more difficult to put right. Perhaps the target is so unrealistic that a short-fall is inevitable. Perhaps an increase in friction in the system is absorbing too much energy. Such friction could arise from personality clash, from communication breakdown, from ineffective delivery, from customer resistance to price changes or from competitive pressure. The important point is to diagnose whether the short-fall is due to internal causes or external pressures. The difficulty is that it is usually a mixture of both – in which case it all gets blamed on external causes. Perhaps the design is bad. Perhaps there is a need for secondary targets to sustain motivation.

42 COLLAPSE

In the drawing the arrow moving towards the target suddenly wilts and collapses. When things go badly wrong, is it best to abort the mission, cut one's losses and use the resources more effectively elsewhere, or go on trying? There is a difference between a project which never gets off the ground and one which suddenly goes bad. The natural tendency is to try harder with the project that has gone some distance. Yet it would be possible to argue exactly the opposite case. The project that never got off the ground may need redesigning. The project that has gone quite far has had every chance of success but has failed and therefore has demonstrated its inadequacy. Obviously it is worth trying to pin-point the cause of failure but that is quite independent of the amount of investment that has been made. An expensive project is just as likely to be in error as a cheap one. An expensive mistake is an expensive mistake – it is not less of a mistake because the money involved inclines us to justify it or seek to put it right.

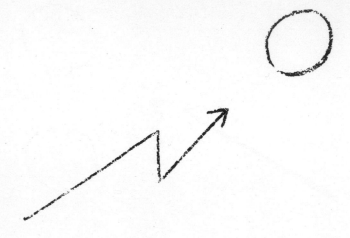

43 RECOVERY

The difference between a bullet and a rocket is that ground control can alter the course of the rocket whilst it is still in flight. The drawing suggests a temporary problem or glitch which has threatened the mission. Matters are put right and the rocket is put back on course for the target. Rigid plans that only work if they are adhered to at every step rarely provide the means for getting back on target once a significant deviation has occurred. Usually far too little design effort is put into 'getting back on target'. Planners design the optimum plans for optimum conditions. A car manufacturer does not design for failure because he believes that his cars will not fail. If a planner thinks his plan is weak at some point he attempts to design out that weakness. But this is not good enough. There needs to be a specific recovery procedure so that if the aim is badly lost it can be recovered again. There needs to be design for repairs as well as design for performance. Who is best able to see the overall picture: the people in the rocket or ground control? Who is best able to put things back on course: the operating unit or central control? The answer will vary from organisation to organisation.

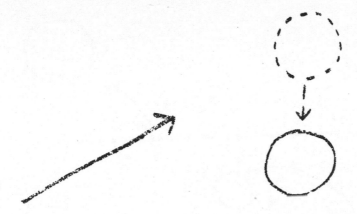

44 SHIFTING TARGET

What happens when the target shifts? It would be more correct to say that something which was used as the target has changed, for the 'target' is a subjective designation and does not change until management decides to change it. Thus a certain sales figure may remain as the target but the spending habits of the income group from which the sales were to come may have shifted. In the US, sales of micro-computers were first aimed at home users. Suddenly it was realised that the main buyers were small businessmen. The reality behind the target had shifted. How much flexibility is there to follow a shifting target? With the micro-computers it meant different software, different machines (at a higher price) and different sales methods: rather large changes. To keep shifting the target all the time makes life impossible and a sort of random walk develops. The difficulty is to determine when a radical shift is required. Tinkering is not much use. The important point is that targets do not shift – they have to be shifted to match the reality that has shifted.

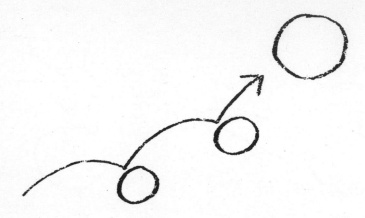

45 INTERMEDIATE TARGETS

The analogy of a gun breaks down badly when we come to consider intermediate targets as shown in the drawing. The rocket analogy still holds up because there are definite stages in the flight of a rocket. Intermediate targets may be genuine targets which can be aimed for in their own right or they may be spurious targets if they are just subdivisions of the journey to the main target. Flying from London to Los Angeles I could make New York a genuine intermediate target by taking a stop-over or I could simply score the half-way mark on the total journey. The advantage of a genuine intermediate target is that, for a while, it becomes an aim in itself. The route to this intermediate target may be quite different from the route that would have led to the ultimate target. For example I might have chosen to go by ship to New York. This would not have been part of the usual flight to Los Angeles. It is important to keep this in mind when setting up intermediate targets. They should be much more than the over-all journey broken down into smaller sections. The intermediate targets should be destinations in their own right – so long as they offer a good starting point for the next stage.

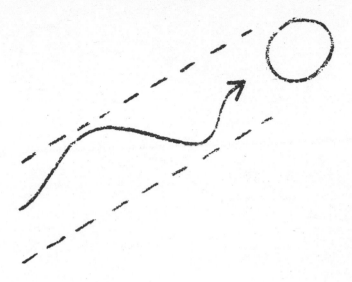

46 GUIDELINES

The difference between tactics and strategy is that tactics covers what you need to do at the moment and strategy provides the broad guidelines that determine over-all direction. The drawing suggests that instead of a constant aim that is on target at every moment, there can be broad guidelines with considerable flexibility of direction between them. Once the guidelines have been set up we can look at them instead of at the target. In essence we acquire guidelines for judgement and decision. How detailed do the guidelines have to be? Sometimes they become so detailed that there is a handbook of practices and procedures that lays down what must be done under all circumstances. At other times they are so vague that almost anything can be interpreted as falling within the guidelines (rather like the very broad articles of association of a company). Detailed guidelines defeat the very purpose of guidelines, which is to allow considerable local flexibility and adjustment. Guidelines that are too vague are not guidelines at all. As with so many things the useful point is between the extremes.

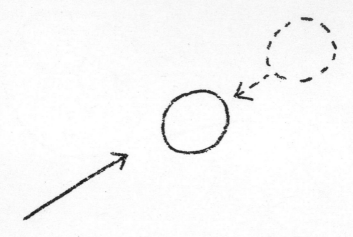

47 BRING THE TARGET NEARER

One way of making sure you hit the target more often is to bring the target nearer. How remote should a target be? With direction targets it does not matter since we do not expect to get there. With feedback and achievement targets there is a trade-off between the nearness of the target and the irritation of continually having to set new targets. The worst target of all is the one that seems to be near but is forever receding as one gets closer to it. In most cases monthly targets would be better than weekly ones but there are many exceptions. What matters more than time is the number of transactions that take place. A salesman who makes a large number of sales every day would probably prefer a weekly target to give him a continued sense of achievement. There is much experimentation on letting people set their own targets. It seems that people tend to be more demanding of themselves than they would ever let management be.

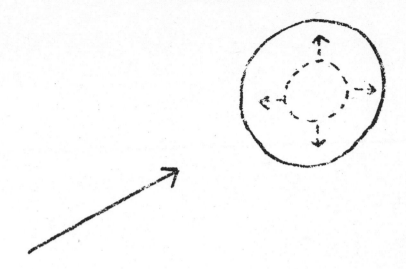

48 BROADEN THE TARGET

There must always be an argument as to whether it is best to have a product that sells to a wide market or one that sells to a specific market sector. The latter allows more focused advertising and distribution and probably higher margins. The trap is that we assume that a broad market means a less specialised product at a low price. But it does not have to be so. The very successful Dexion slotted angle iron appealed to a very broad market (anyone whose used storage) yet it was specialised for the job it had to do and sold at a good price. It is a fatal error to assume that lowering the price makes an indifferent product saleable to a general market. Another fatal error is to assume that a product with general appeal should be marketed broadly (with consequent high costs of promotion). The seller can still choose to market the product in a very focused area – as was so successfully done with the 'four-walling' concept for marketing movie films. This involved focusing on medium-sized towns one after another and blitzing them with publicity.

PROBLEM-SOLVING

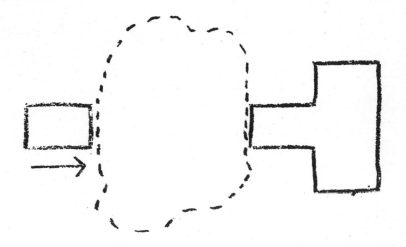

49 INFORMATION AND PROBLEM-SOLVING

The drawing shows a defined problem solution and a defined starting point. In between there is a vague area that needs forming into a track from the starting point to the solution. There is no substitute for information and many problems can be solved just by making an effort to find the right information (market research, production costs, financing availability). There are situations, however, where information will not do our thinking for us. Information by itself will not generate ideas. Ideas are organisations of information that the human mind chooses to put together in a particular way. The concept behind any business is an idea. Any strategy is an idea.

Problem-solving can require ideas as much as it does information. The unfortunate thing is that problem solvers tend to polarise into two groups: the information gatherers who are not very comfortable with ideas, and the idea people who think they do not need information. In tackling a problem it is useful to gather as much information as possible and then to decide whether the solution is going to depend on more information or on a new idea.

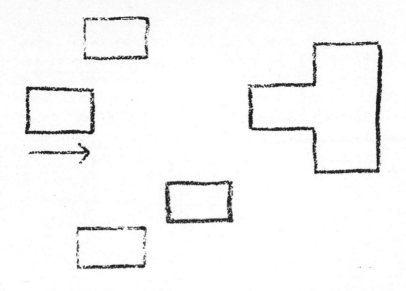

50 THE FACTORS INVOLVED

The drawing suggests the many factors that have to be taken into consideration when setting out to solve a problem. In school textbooks a certain amount of information is given, for example in a maths problem. The pupil knows that all the information required has been given to him. He also knows that he is supposed to use all the information given. So he sets about sorting it out. This idiom encourages the very bad habit of believing that life is going to be as neatly packaged as a school textbook. It is not. In real life it is up to the problem-solver to search around and find the factors that should be taken into consideration and the ones that can safely be left out. In one of my books I gave more information than was needed to solve a particular problem. I got howls of protest from readers who thought that I was deliberately misleading them. The first step in problem-solving is to form some idea (it cannot be definite) as to the factors that really are involved and those that can be ignored. Some ruthlessness may be needed.

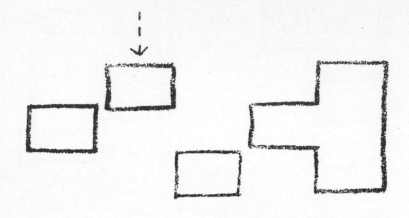

51 COMBINING ELEMENTS

We would all be much happier if real life problem-solving was like assembling the pieces of a jigsaw puzzle. We would search for the defined pieces and then put them together in the proper order as suggested in the drawing. In some cases this is certainly possible. In areas where the basic laws of action are known (parts of chemistry, physics, engineering, etc.) this can be done. An engineer knows how different elements will behave and can combine them to give a desired effect. If he does this easily enough we probably would not bother to call it a 'problem', but in a sense it is. In other areas, such as economics, consumer behaviour or labour relations, the laws of action are far less known and far less reliable. The elements are also not clearly defined. We cannot, for example, take for granted that raising a person's wages will make him work harder. Nor can an economist take it for granted that inflation will make people save more (in the US they save less). Yet to have any confidence in our solution we need to combine known segments of action and effect.

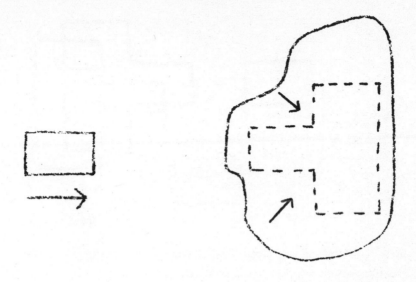

52 DEFINE THE PROBLEM

Many books on problem solving urge the thinker to define the problem very clearly. Such books state that if a problem is defined correctly then it is easy to solve. This is really rather unfair because the only time we can really define correctly is in hindsight – when we have already found the solution and are merely inventing a definition that would have led us there! In spite of this we do need to make an effort to define the problem. Since we are unlikely to find the best definition we should try defining the problem in alternative ways. At the very least this habit will get us out of a rigid frame of mind which only looks at the problem in a way determined by experience. There is no doubt that some problems can be solved with ease if only we can get to look at them in a different way. But finding that different way is not so easy. That is where lateral thinking can come in useful.

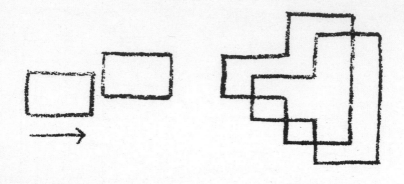

53 CONFUSION

In a problem-solving discussion it often becomes clear that the people present are all trying to solve slightly different problems. Each of these problems is similar enough to fall under the same broad heading but distinct enough to create confusion as the problem-solving proceeds. It is well worth pausing from time to time to clarify what problem each person thinks he or she is solving. For example in an advertising agency discussion about a new campaign to revive a soft drink, one person might be trying to solve the problem of how an old drink can be called 'new' in any sense; another person might be trying to solve the problem of how 'old' can be made appealing; and a third person might be trying to solve the problem of designing a theme that will sell not to the public but to the marketing manager who has to okay the campaign. Having the same general intention is not the same as trying to solve the same problem. The difficulty only arises when there is communication. Different people solving slightly different problems in separate rooms create no difficulty – until they come to communicate their solutions, which are assumed to be for the same problem.

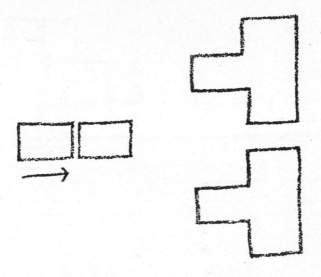

54 CONTRADICTION

There are some problems which are set up to be impossible to solve. It is not possible to go in two different directions at the same time. For example it may not be possible to design a car that is heavier and uses less fuel. It may not be possible to lower wages and raise motivation at the same time. It may not be possible to spend less on promotion and to increase the market share. It is worth spending some thinking time even on such apparent contradictions, but it is also worth examining problems to see whether they are difficult to solve simply because they demand the satisfaction of opposites at the same time. There is no reason why problems should be harder than they already are. Dropping some requirement may make the problem much easier to solve. If this is the case (and it can be tried with dropping several requirements each in turn) then the requirement should be examined to see if it was essential in the first place. There is no limit to the wants we can express in language and hence we may well set up problems that are impossible to solve because they require the resolution of contradictions.

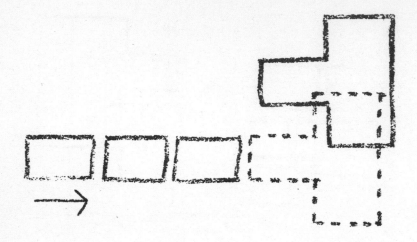

55 SOLVING THE WRONG PROBLEM

The drawing suggests the successful completion of a path from the starting point to the solution of the problem. Unfortunately it seems to be the wrong problem. Most motorists know that it is possible to feel absolutely certain what the matter is with the engine and to put that right only to find that the car still does not start. We are back again with the school textbook idiom. In the textbook situation we solve the problem that is put in front of us. In real life we may solve the problem that seems to confront us only to find that it is not the most important problem. In industry it often happens that a great deal of thought goes into the design of a project, when the real problem is finding the right person to run the project. If the right person can be found then much of the detailed work can be delegated to him. Cost-saving exercises may not be tackling the real problem which is the need for a structural change.

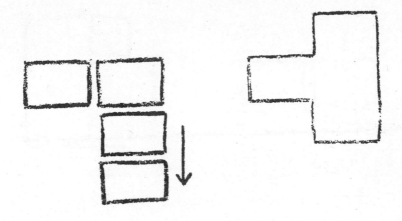

56 DIVERSION

When we solve a problem by combining different elements of known action we sometimes get carried away. Certain of the elements combine so naturally and with so powerful an effect that we pursue that path of combination as a path in its own right and forget about the problem we are trying to solve. That is the reasoning behind the pleas for some allocation of R & D funds to basic research where this sort of behaviour would be encouraged (the following up of leads for their own sake). In other situations, however, the temptation can be disastrous. The problem-solver gets carried away by the interest of the idea. In the end he presents it as a solution to the problem which he had been set but it is really nothing of the sort. It is an interesting idea but not a solution to the problem. Even if it is a sort of solution to the problem it is unlikely to be the simplest or the cheapest. This sort of thing happens very often when a new data-processing system is to be installed to fulfil a particular task. In the end an expensive system is installed not to fulfil the task but to do lots of other fascinating things that do not need doing.

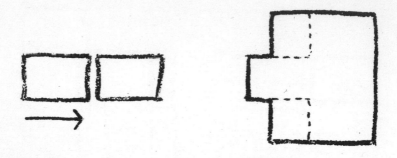

57 AN APPROXIMATE SOLUTION

How exact does the solution really have to be? Is an approximate solution usable? What is the trade-off in terms of cost and time between an exact solution and an approximate one? This is somewhat like making the target broader so that it becomes easier to hit. In mathematics approximations are very often used in order to give the rough shape of the solution. For some purposes this may be enough. We should not seek for precision where precision is an unnecessary and costly luxury. The other reason for looking for an approximate solution is that once it has been found such an approximate solution can then be worked upon and modified to give a much better solution. The mind finds it much easier to work upon something than to cast around in a search. Once the approximate solution has been found then it is no longer a problem situation but a design situation: how can the solution be designed in a better way?

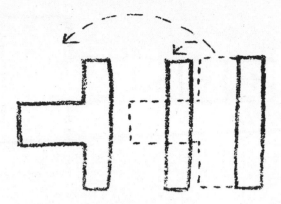

58 BREAK DOWN THE PROBLEM

The drawing suggests how the problem might be broken down into components. Instead of trying to solve the problem all at once there is an attempt to create sub-problems. For example in trying to increase the fuel efficiency of a car we might create the following sub-problems: better fuel consumption in the cylinder; better timing of ignition; use of exhaust gas heat; reduction of weight of body; less fuel consumption for air conditioners, etc. Each of these problems could in turn be broken down into sub-problems. For example the reduction of body weight could lead to a problem of re-design of shape but also to one of substituting plastics for metal. The problem of air resistance could be broken down into shape and surface effects. A word of caution is required because if everyone is working on a sub-problem then it becomes difficult to tackle the whole problem in a novel way. In a sense the breakdown of a problem is always based on the old way of looking at the problem.

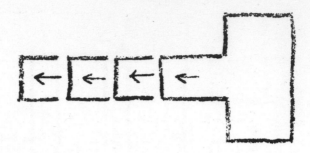

59 WORKING BACKWARDS

One of the most powerful problem-solving methods is to work backwards from the hoped-for solution. It is not unlike end-play in chess 'What preceding state could have led to this position; what pre-preceding states could have led to that state, etc.?' The possible states preceding the solution-state are taken as destinations and we look for states that might have preceded each of them... and so on back, until we are within range of where we start. Imagine a car journey from Edinburgh to London. London is the destination so we work backwards from London. 'If only I could get to Hatfield then the journey from there to London is easy. Now I could get to Hatfield very easily from Baldock, so now I need to get to Baldock...' all the way back to Edinburgh. Although the process is powerful it is by no means easy to use because it requires a very great deal of imagination and conceptual skill. The steps must be small and concrete. It is also necessary to define the desired end-state very clearly.

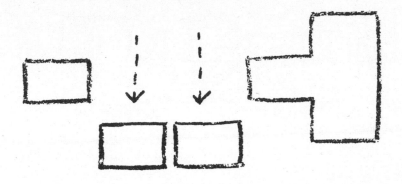

60 SELF-CREATED PROBLEMS

These problems appear to be real enough and to be indistinguishable from other problems but in fact they have only been created by ourselves. They have been created because we have chosen to look at a situation in a certain way or we have chosen to treat as a problem something which is merely a change. The clarifying question is: 'Is this really a problem or am I just choosing to look at it as a problem?' A problem may arise as a result of a change we have made somewhere else. Or it may arise because we are pursuing a particular path and if we went back upstream we could avoid the problem instead of trying to solve it. If you come to an obstruction in a road you can seek to circumvent it or you can retrace your journey to the nearest fork and avoid that road altogether. Once again it is a matter of escaping from the textbook idiom which assumes that presented problems have to be solved. They do not have to be solved if they can be avoided.

OPPORTUNITIES

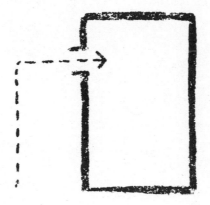

61 OPPORTUNITIES

Although opportunities are so obviously different from problems there is a style of management thinking which equates the two by broadening the definition of a 'problem' to include anything you might want to achieve. This is semantic nonsense and does great harm to management thinking. With a problem we look for a solution. With an opportunity we look for benefits. With a problem we know where we want to end up. With an opportunity we do not know exactly where we want to go until we have found it. Business schools teach problem-solving. Experience teaches problem-solving to rising executives because there are always enough urgent problems to be tackled and promotion comes to those who seem good at tackling them.

As a result of all this, opportunity-thinking is neglected and is left to individual entrepreneurs who have to answer to nobody but themselves. We need to pay as much deliberate attention to opportunity-seeking as we do to problem-solving. The box shown in the drawing is an opportunity space. That is to say it is a secret garden. It is a perceptual garden in which there are goodies to be picked – once the garden has been entered. It is entered by looking for the entrance: by looking for opportunity.

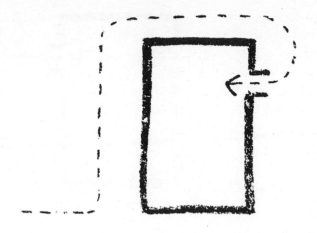

62 HIDDEN OPPORTUNITY

The entrance to the 'opportunity garden' is less obvious than in the first drawing. Opportunities range from those which are more or less obvious to everyone to those which are only spotted by someone who makes the conceptual breakthrough. There are certain opportunities that only occur to organisations with the necessary technical competence, market position or trading relationships. There are others which are open to anyone who has the ingenuity to think of them. Sometimes an opportunity is so obvious to the person who has thought of it that he cannot imagine how it is not equally obvious to everyone else. In hindsight the trading stamps idea was a brilliant concept. So was Laker's concept of cheap but regular air travel. Are we better off searching for the hidden opportunities or spotting the obvious ones early enough? Both strategies are right: the first for individuals and the second for larger organisations.

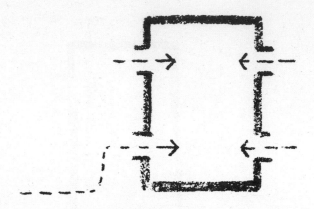

63 CROWDED OPPORTUNITY SPACE

The second-in-the-field and the 'me-too' people usually do very well. They do not have the ego-satisfaction of having thought up a brand new idea but in practical terms they do well. The pioneer has developed the field and born the development costs. Early snags have been ironed out. Legal questions have been settled. The new product has moved from a novelty to a buying habit. Even when a new field seems overcrowded there is usually good business still to be had because the field itself expands under the pressure of the newcomers as they advertise to gain market share. Kodak's entry into the instant camera business increased the business of Polaroid because Kodak had to advertise its way in and so increased the total market. There always seems to be room for a new maker of trainers. It is only in the fashion or fad field that the latercomers get badly burned. They enter at the peak and like those who buy shares at their peak they suffer badly. The 'me-too' opportunity should not be ignored just because of its lack of creativity.

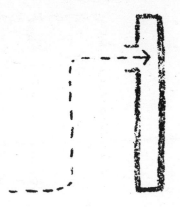

64 THE SHALLOW OPPORTUNITY

From the outside it looks the same as the broader opportunity garden, but once through the gates the entrant sees that it is only a narrow strip. A shallow opportunity is one that seems attractive at first sight. The concept is good and original – but the volume or margins simply are not there. It could be that the market is too small. It could also be that the chain of distribution is so complicated that margins are pared to nothing. The sheer ingenuity of an opportunity idea should not bedazzle the entrepreneur to the extent that he fails to do his sums and work out the profitability of the venture. On the other hand there is shallow and shallow. What is a shallow opportunity to a large corporation may offer a substantial opportunity to a smaller concern. That is the basis of the famous 'niche' strategy which means that you secure for yourself a useful market by doing something which the big boys find uneconomical to do at the price you can manage.

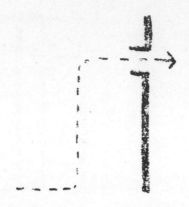

65 FALSE OPPORTUNITY

Many people wake up in the night with a wonderful 'eureka' idea which does not stand up to examination in the cold light of morning. The sudden snapping together of two lines of thought gives a feeling of insight or discovery. It can be immensely useful – and that is what is looked for with lateral thinking – or it can be false. The clever trader secures his buyer before he makes his purchase. The foolish trader is tempted by a bargain price and then scurries around trying to find a buyer for his bargains. The psychology of January sales depends on the attractiveness of false opportunities to enough people. The success of get-rich-quick schemes and some of the earlier pyramid ventures depend on the same thing. An opportunity should never be judged by the size of the potential gains but by the likelihood of those gains. Yet human psychology does not work that way. Human psychology reckons that a 1 per cent chance of a $1 million dollar gain is as real as a 100 per cent chance of $1,000 gain. That may work for a lottery system where the buyer buys the fun of expectation but it does not – or should not – apply to opportunities.

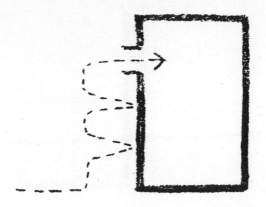

66 SENSING AN OPPORTUNITY

Before an opportunity is actually found there is usually a pre-
liminary sense that there is an opportunity somewhere in the
area. It is not unlike the feeling a good scientist gets when he
senses he is within range of something interesting. This sense is
strong enough to motivate a succession of attempts to find what
is interesting. In the same way a general sensing of an opportunity 'somewhere in the neighbourhood' can fuel a succession
of tries as suggested in the drawing. Failure to find the right
concept at the first attempt simply leads to a second attempt
and a third attempt. Such persistence is not easy because there
is nothing to go on except the general hunch that there ought
to be an opportunity somewhere about. Although the early
attempts may be conceptual failures there is a growing knowledge of the field so that when the right idea is found it can be
more easily recognised. Many people stare good opportunities
in the face but are unable to recognise them because they do
not know enough about the field.

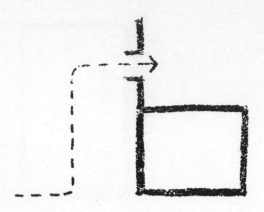

67 FALSE ENTRY

There is a well known phrase: 'Just because I'm paranoid it doesn't mean that people are not persecuting me.' The same thing can apply to opportunities. Just because there is a real opportunity area does not mean that all entries into the area are likely to be successful. The drawing shows both a real opportunity area and also a false entry. Recognising an opportunity area is not quite the same as putting together a specific concept and a plan of operating. It is a nice feeling to be in a candy store but until you decide what you want and buy it the nice feeling does not turn into a nice taste. It may be enough for an investment trust to tempt investors by describing the opportunity area in broad terms, and inasmuch as this temptation continues to work then the early investors can sell out at a profit to the later ones. But for other people an opportunity is only an opportunity when there is a workable concept that is being worked.

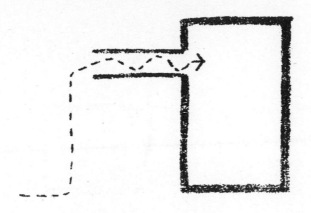

68 DELAYED REWARD

How long do you pursue a tempting idea before operating a 'cut-off'? As long as the enthusiasm, temptation or resources last. How deep do you drill an oil well? On the whole we expect opportunities to start paying off very quickly. Otherwise we begin to doubt the concept. The very concept of an opportunity suggests early and large rewards. If this were not so the risk of doing something new would not be justified. Mere faith in an idea can only sustain it for a limited time especially when others are required to act upon that faith. No doubt there are many inadequately pursued opportunities around that could be revived and worked through more thoroughly. I have often suggested that a good place to look for worthwhile ideas is in the bankruptcy fields, for failure can be due to so many causes other than the failure of the basic concept (poor management, cash-flow problems, dainty investors, competition at the time, technical problems, etc.). In the oil world there is a great opportunity in working out a tertiary recovery method from used-up fields. Perhaps that principle could be applied to other opportunity areas.

PEOPLE

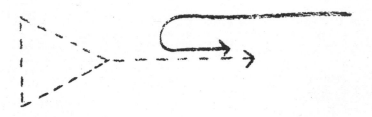

69 APPROVAL

The triangle represents other people. The thrust of activity and motivation follows the direction of the apex of the triangle. The broken arrow represents output or work effort. The heavy line represents management. Approval is given for something that has been done so the management arrow is somewhat behind the broken arrow. Is it a sort of bonus approval for something that has been done particularly well or approval for an ordinary job well done? Is it paternalistic approval bestowed whether it is really deserved or not, or acknowledgement of output targets that are routinely reached. Most psychologists are agreed that recognition and approval can be powerful motivators. What is less agreed upon is whether the reward should be given for routine adequacy or for extra special effort. Does a reward become devalued if it is given routinely? The answer seems to be that it does not. There is even a suggestion that rewards which are routine and expected may be more motivating than the ones given only for extra special effort. The two are not mutually exclusive. The British army has always given campaign medals which are rewards for just being there and doing an ordinary job, and special medals for gallantry beyond the call of duty.

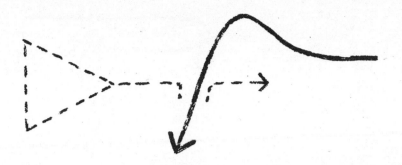

70 DISAPPROVAL

The heavy arrow smashes across and breaks the line of activity. The effect is exaggerated to indicate heavy handed disapproval. Some people seem able to indicate disapproval without causing offence whilst others cause resentment even with the mildest expression of dissatisfaction. It may be the choice of words or it may be the respect that is accorded to the disapprover. There are many standard ways of making disapproval obvious in an oblique way (not up to quota, not up to standard, disappointing, seem unable to match performance of competitor, there must be a problem somewhere, etc.) which may be less offensive than the direct method – but may also be less effective. It should be possible to tell someone who is being paid to do a job that the job is not being done well enough. The basis for the complaint needs to be honest. The general use of disapproval in order to keep people on their toes tends to be counterproductive after a time. Where the fault lies with the structure of the job there is little point in blaming the holder of the job. The holder could, of course be asked for suggestions on redesigning the job.

71 LEADERSHIP

It hardly needs saying that leadership is from the front – as suggested by the arrow in the drawing. Yet many people regard leadership in a different way. To these people leadership is like driving a team of horses. You sit behind the horses, hold the reins and do the navigating. Control is not the same as leadership. Control can approximate the effects of leadership only with people who are highly trained, docile and energetic all at the same time. It is a combination that is just possible but rare. Is leadership a natural quality or can it be learned? It does not really matter so long as we accept both points of view. In practice that means keeping an eye out for leadership qualities and sometimes selecting on that basis and, at the same time, encouraging the absorption of certain leadership precepts by those who do not seem to possess them in a natural way. Some cooks are born great, others have their natural skill improved by training, yet others train hard enough to make up for a lack of natural talent.

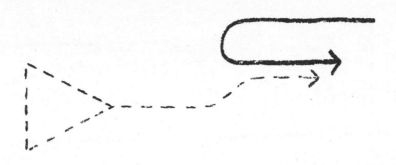

72 INSTRUCTION

Instruction is a sort of specific leadership. The drawing suggests that the broken arrow rises to follow the management arrow. The training or instruction has been successful. Training programmes are neutral. They benefit management but they are not undertaken to please management. They should be designed to add skills to the person taking the training even if some of those skills are broader than those actually required for the task. There is always a case for making training rather broader than task-instruction. If training succeeds in raising the 'operating intelligence' in a broader way, then the spin-off from this will have benefits elsewhere. The strict 'bottom line' approach to training is somewhat short-sighted. Training is a sort of fuel, not just a bag of tricks that can be applied.

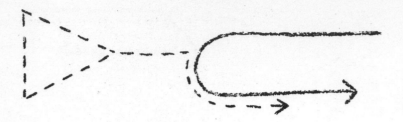

73 DEMAND

The contrast between instruction and demand should be clear from the drawings. In the demand drawing the broken line is pushed to a different level instead of being drawn to it. As an operating strategy 'demand' cannot be seen in isolation. It has to be seen in the climate, culture or context of an organisation. If 'demand' is an accepted idiom then it can work quite well. There are people who seem to like a tightly structured organisation where initiative is replaced by demand. Such people like to know where they are. They like to carry out coherent and organised tasks. It is often claimed that children crave discipline because without it they are overloaded with judgements, decisions and opportunities. Freedom is a heavy taskmaster for those awake enough to appreciate it. When does a request become a 'demand'? When automatic compliance is expected. In that case an aggressive demand defeats its own purpose for the use of aggression to ensure compliance and suggests that compliance is not really expected.

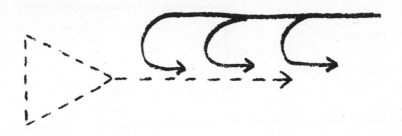

74 COAXING

Animal trainers have always used a coaxing method. The required action is broken down into small segments and a reward is given when the next segment of action is correctly performed – even if this is done by chance. Gradually the whole sequence of action is learned in a painless manner. The behavioural psychologists have applied this 'shaping' method to human behaviour. It does work and its very success attaches to the method the stigma of manipulation. Coaxing is a less effective – and therefore more acceptable – method of achieving similar results. The main elements are attention and reward. The attention needs to be constant and the rewards are given frequently, not just at the end. This close attention is itself the major motivator and reward. The small incremental steps are not threatening. The major problem with the method is that it takes a great deal of time, attention and patience. The animal trainer has plenty of each.

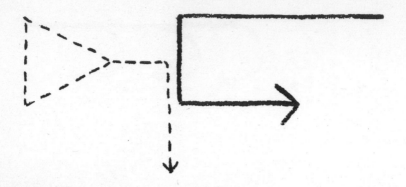

75 BLOCKING

The important point in the drawing is that the direction of the broken arrow has been permanently altered through the temporary insertion of a block. We tend to feel that things are reversible: the effect of reward will wear off; the effect of punishment will wear off. This is probably true but context changes can be permanent. Someone who suggests a new idea only to have it squashed may deduce that the context is not one for putting forward ideas. He may never put forward another idea. He senses that the rules of the game exclude putting forward idea. Learning the 'rules of the game' is a very subtle and permanent process. Children at school quickly learn the rules of the school game and of the 'mates game'. Once learned the rules are almost impossible to change. That is why what may at first seem to be a casual incident can have lasting effects. It is sometimes useful to put oneself in the shoes of another person. The rules of the game are rather more specific than the culture of an organisation. Whereas most learning requires a lot of repetition, learning the rules of the game happens very fast.

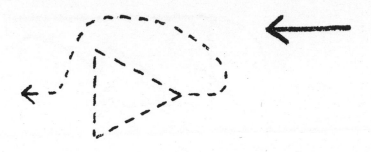

76 TURN-OFF

The drawing hardly needs any explanation. The baddy in a pantomime is hated but loved at the same time. To be effective there is certainly no need for management to be loved in a 'warm' sort of way. That sort of relationship would be very difficult to sustain or to generalise beyond one or two individuals. Management can be hated and still be effective. The 'turn-off' is, however, something different. It is a mixture of boredom, resentment, lack of interest, and even contempt. The boredom is probably the most active ingredient. Contrary to what some people suppose, boredom is a strong emotion not just a matter of apathy and inertia. Can a turn-off situation be redeemed? Probably, but not without a change in management personnel. That the situation may not be anyone's fault does not mean that no sacrifices are required.

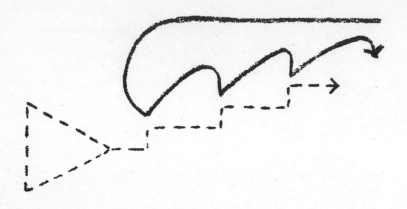

77 MOTIVATION

Motivation is a great catchword. If people are properly motivated they will do anything and enjoy it. The drawing suggests
the movement to higher and higher levels of productive output
through incentives offered in order to raise output at each step.
There is a sort of upward ratchet effect where each achievement level becomes the baseline for the next change. The
effect is somewhat idealistic and could only be achieved where
motivation and performance were at a very low level to begin
with. Should motivation be applied in bursts or as a continuous background? If the system is designed to encompass both
types then both types can be used. The successful 'buck-a-day'
cost-cutting programme that is used in the USA works because
the strong motivation is applied for a short time. In addition
to changes in structure and general climate there is a place for
short bursts of motivational effort. These should take some
practical form rather than plain exhortation.

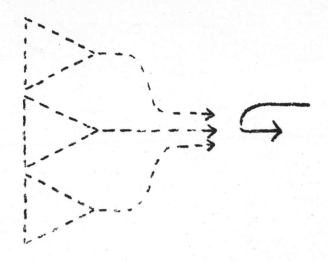

78 ORGANISATION

Groups are said to work because the group members can now react to each other instead of just reacting to management. In reacting to each other they may develop attitudes and habits similar to the ones desired by management. The Japanese quality-circle style has become popular outside Japan because it seems to offer a tried framework for this sort of group motivation. The real value of the method is seen to lie in its motivating effect more than in the changes in production methods. The success of the groups seems to depend not so much on the Japanese 'group culture' but on the motivating effect of any group. Negative attitudes tend to spread more easily amongst individuals than from group to group because members of a group can argue more effectively amongst themselves than can an individual. It is also possible that the leadership qualities demanded by a group are less exacting than those required by a collection of individuals. Individuals have to derive all their sustenance from a leader. Group members derive some of it from each other.

CHANGE

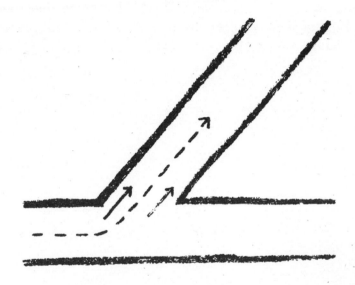

SIGN-POSTS

This shows change by sign-posting the new route and leaving the old route intact. People are supposed to observe the sign-posts and obey the instructions. It is possibly the least effective method of change because it depends on two steps both of which are unnatural. The first is that people should read sign-posts when they have no reason for doing so (the reason is the management's) and the second is that they should be willing – and should remember – to follow the instructions. At best it is likely to lead to confusion as some people follow the new route and others hang on to the old one. The method can work if there is a long time for the changeover, if both channels can be kept open and if it does not matter that the two systems are being used haphazardly. In many cases there may be no choice. The success of the operation depends on how effective the communication system (symbolised by the signposts) is and how the new channel compares to the old one in terms of convenience. If the new system does offer real advantages then peer-group pressure might take over after a time and accelerate the change-over.

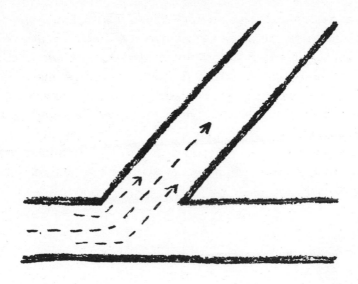

80 BELL-WETHERS

Individuals or small groups are carefully trained in the new methods and then put back into their usual working positions. They are supposed to lead the change both by example and by exhortation. They are also in a position to explain the new methods and to communicate their virtues. It is an effective method especially if the change affects daily life so that the trained group can be seen to operate differently and can be asked for advice frequently. With procedures that are only used occasionally it is less likely to be successful and the trained group may even forget their training. By creating the élite trained group there is a small danger of polarising opinion into those who favour the change and those who set out to resist it. Some people resent having to ask advice about something which they have always managed quite competently. Much also depends on the effectiveness of the training. If there are some who have misunderstood the system amongst the trained group then this misunderstanding will spread and become difficult to eradicate. Back-up methods are needed in addition.

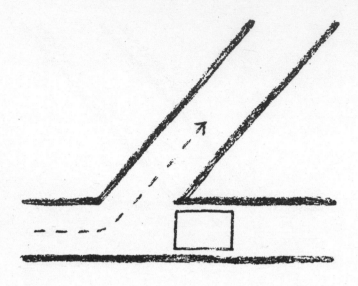

81 BLOCK THE OLD ROUTE

The old route is quite simply blocked off. The old forms are discontinued. People are forced to choose the new route. In some situations this type of abrupt and complete switch-over is necessary since it is not possible to have both old and new methods running side by side (for example in switching over from driving on one side of the road to the other as in Sweden). If confusion and resentment are to be avoided the change-over must be simple to understand and must have been heralded so far in advance that it is almost an anti-climax when it finally comes. On the whole changing behaviour patterns by blocking off existing patterns is the least effective method because blocking one pattern does not by itself create a new one. Punishing someone for doing the wrong thing may inhibit him from that action but does not establish a better pattern. The most effective form of block is 'absence'. If there are no old forms around they cannot be used. Where a 'no entry' sign is placed on the old behaviour it is much less likely to work because the temptation of the familiar path is too strong.

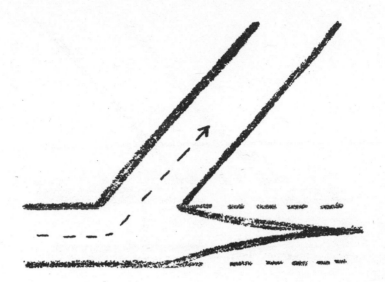

82 ATROPHY

Disuse is the natural way to kill off an old behaviour pattern. The pattern is allowed to atrophy through disuse. Disuse comes about if there is a much more attractive competing pattern or if the old pattern becomes inconvenient, tiresome or too much bother. Inconvenience is a much stronger deterrent than prohibition. Laziness is one of the more effective ways of changing behaviour. The old patterns are allowed to persist but are made progressively more inconvenient. If – as happens too often – the new methods are even more inconvenient than the old then a change-over is difficult, because to the basic inconvenience of the new pattern must be added the inconvenience of learning it. On the whole we are too ashamed to use inconvenience as a way of changing behaviour because it seems dishonest and inefficient. We are ashamed to deliberately make a system so inconvenient that people will stop using it. We just hope it will happen by itself. The great advantage of the atrophy system is that once a pattern has atrophied away it is extremely unlikely ever to revive.

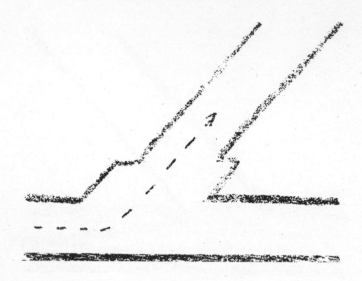

83 TEMPTATION

The new route of pattern is made to seem very attractive in contrast to the old – simpler and more convenient. In the drawing this is indicated by the much greater width of the new pattern. It is true that the great width is only to be found in the first part of the new route but that is enough. All that is required is that the initial comparison should clearly favour the change-over. Once the change-over has been made it may be impossible to sustain the extra attractiveness. This is not cheating but acknowledging that the change-over period is one of difficulty and strain and should be made as attractive as possible. Leaving the security of a familiar situation for an unknown situation is difficult enough. Making the new situation attractive is not the same as making it seem attractive. It really should be attractive in the initial stages. We hope to sell goods by packaging them attractively. We spend far too little time on the packaging of change for fear of misleading people. In fact it is just as misleading to ignore the packaging and expect someone to assess the new situation without any help. If you knew nothing about chocolate and it was not wrapped would you ever buy it?

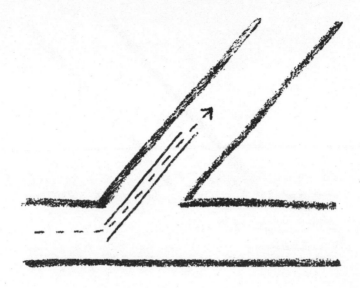

84 STAGED TRANSITION

The drawing suggests that the switch to the new route is taken in stages. Small channels are built to divert some of the traffic to the new route. There is no attempt to bring about a complete switch-over. In practice this might mean changing one department at a time. The advantage of the method is that experience with the change procedure accumulates. The snags can be ironed out at an early stage. Those who have already changed over can help those about to change over. The first group to change have the motivation of being pioneers. The change becomes easier and easier and when the mid-point is passed those who have been left behind with the old method are only too eager to catch up with their colleagues. New uniforms are usually introduced in this way. Before it becomes threatening, the strangeness of the new wears off. The eventual change-over becomes a matter of routine. The staged process allows the majority to watch the change without having to be involved in it for some time. The same principle can be applied to behaviour patterns. A person role-plays the new pattern now and again – and then more often.

85 TRANSITION CHANNEL

As the drawing suggests a specific transition channel is designed to lead the traffic into the new route. This is designed for the purpose of transition only. The new method is designed to be permanent but the transition channel is designed to be transitory. There can therefore be built into the design of this channel features that could not be built into a permanent method. As mentioned elsewhere the specific design of transition methods gets too little attention. We assume that it is enough that the new way will prove better than the old way once it has been tried for sometime. This may well be so but it may never get tried if the transition is too difficult. Furthermore a difficult transition can prejudice the changers against the new method so that they never appreciate its superiority over the old method. In the field of ideas we rarely design transition ideas: ideas that are never meant to be permanent. We see nothing wrong in designing vehicles that are intended for motion but we feel it wrong to design ideas that are also intended for motion. We feel we have to deal in truth and truth is static.

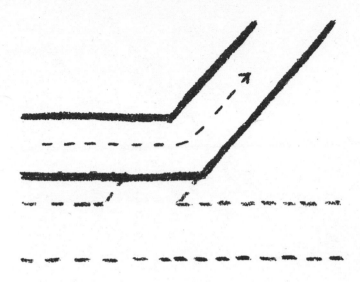

86 NEW ENTRY POINT

Instead of trying to switch people from the old track we start afresh and just ignore the old track. We shut down the old plant and start afresh somewhere else with a new labour force. In the building trade it is well known that the cost of building a new building may be less than the cost of modifying an old one. Perhaps we try too hard to modify because we feel that evolution should be a continuous process. In the design world old designs become more and more laboured and more and more mannered. Then quite suddenly a new design starts up. It does not arise from the old style but in opposition to it. If change becomes too complicated we should call it something else. Instead of trying to change old attitudes we can set out to design new ones which are not descendants of the old ones. Usually we seek to maintain the bridge from the old to the new on the grounds that this gives security. It is just possible that it does exactly the opposite. There may be more security in hanging on to the old and acquiring something new as well.

OBJECTIVES

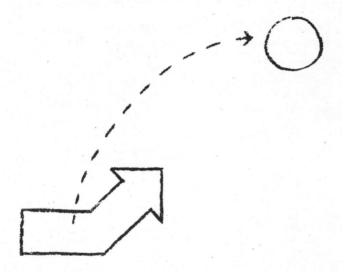

87 SETTING AN OBJECTIVE

We take it for granted that organisations should have objectives. We take it for granted that individual departments and even individual managers should have objectives. Management by objectives is a well-known management technique. But why? Because if we do not have objectives we drift or stagnate or follow every temptation. Much of this takes change or growth for granted. If you are going somewhere then you have to know where you are going in order to point in the right direction. Yet there are many instances where continued competent survival is objective enough. A large retail chain may want to expand and build more stores or it may be content with its current size since all the most profitable regions are covered. Replacing older stores with new ones is part of maintenance. Being alert to new trends, watching the costs and day-to-day profitability may be enough. A trading company may have the general objective of surviving and making good deals. When we think of objectives we tend to think of objectives for growth and change. Objectives concerned with maintenance or good housekeeping need a different description.

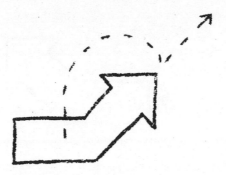

88 MOMENTUM

The drawing suggests that no specific objective has been set. The momentum of the organisation is its own objective. The organisation is pointing in a direction and the momentum keeps it going in that direction. In the days of the conglomerates momentum kept them going even though each step was rationalised after it had been made. Property companies keep going impelled by their momentum and the opportunities that are offered to them. Success, market valuation and cash flow provide a powerful momentum. Direction is determined not by an objective but by the nature of the organisation and the field in which it operates. Pseudo-objectives may be set in terms of size and assets but they are descriptions of the general intention to keep going and getting bigger. If you are in a dealing situation and each deal made is a sound one then momentum may be enough. Indeed it could be argued that setting objectives may put the corporation off course by diverting attention from moment-to-moment operations to a distant destination.

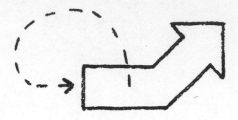

89 REAR-END OBJECTIVES

We think of objectives as a carrot luring an organisation forward. We think of objectives as destinations that are to be reached. In both cases the objective is out in front. If you happen to sit on a drawing pin and jump up the objective is a rear-end one. In other words the objective is to escape from an uncomfortable position rather than to reach a particular destination. Jumping up off a seat is easy enough because almost any action will make things better. With a corporation that is in trouble a lot of actions might make things worse so the natural tendency is to try to escape from the present troubles by setting a specific objective and moving towards that. Unfortunately that may be much too slow. To decide what the company should be like in five years time may not solve a crisis that is looming up next month. That is not to stay that long-term objectives should not be considered in addition to the escape strategy that is being worked upon. It is simply that long-term objectives do not constitute an escape strategy. If banks or outside rescuers are to be involved then they will want to know the long-term prospects and objectives so these cannot be ignored. When you are pulling yourself out of a swamp you do not consult a road map.

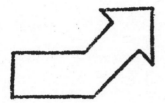

90 SHOPPING

Men go shopping with an objective. They know what they want to buy, rush into the appropriate shop, buy the item and end the shopping. For women shopping seems to be different. They appreciate the effort the manufacturer has gone to in order to produce the goods. They appreciate the trouble taken by the retailer to display the goods. There is no rush. They may have some specific items that are to be bought but they also have a general readiness to look around and be tempted by what they might see. They do not look at everything with a view to buying it. They are prepared to look at something appreciatively without wanting to buy it. If the appreciation is high enough and the price is possible then a purchase results. For some organisations objectives are rather more like a woman shopping than a man shopping. There is a general objective to look around – not a specific objective to look for some particular thing. When an attractive opportunity presents itself then action follows. This is essentially an opportunistic stance as distinct from an opportunity-developing one. But it works.

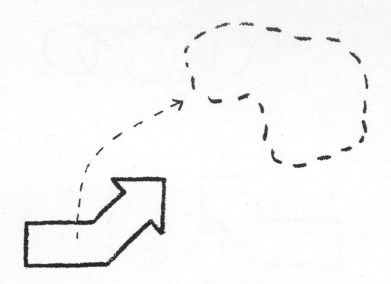

91 VAGUE OBJECTIVES

To have vague objectives is to have the worst of both worlds. There is not the opportunistic freedom of being able to change the direction to follow a temptation, nor is there the firm route-planning that would lead to a specific destination. In practice to have vague objectives will prevent one from doing much and yet not generate positive action. Vague objectives might include maintaining a market share or keeping up with technology or offering good value to the customer. Politicians have to have vague objectives in order to stay in tune with their supporters and circumstances. For a politician to have a clear objective is to offer hostages to his opponents. Any change of direction becomes a retreat or a U-turn. Any pause in progress towards the objective is a matter of reneging on electoral promises. Corporations do not suffer from these constraints. Shareholders and stock analysts want to see action. Action means movement and where there is movement there must at least be a claim that it is movement in a particular direction. At worst a vague objective should be couched in very precise terms. That is a skill for which lawyers are highly paid in another area.

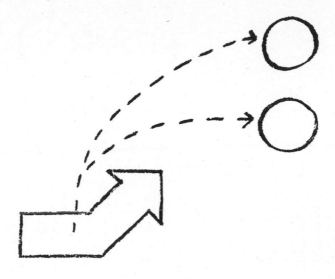

92 ALTERNATIVE OBJECTIVES

Many young women find it possible to love two men simultaneously. They put it down to indecision and the overwhelming charms of both suitors. It could be that it is really a form of fall-back insurance. If you do not know exactly what is going to happen it is well to keep your options open. Military commanders find it essential to have alternative objectives. If one objective proves impossible to achieve or is pre-empted by an enemy move then there is a switch to the other objective. Obviously it is not a matter of pursuing both objectives at the same time. It is more a matter of being in a position to switch if necessary. In contrast, business corporations find it very hard to have alternative objectives. This is because one or other must be better, and pride cannot allow executives to settle for the second best – so why think of it in the first place? If competitors and circumstances are regarded as the 'enemy' then it makes as much sense for a corporation to have alternative objectives as it does for a military commander. A change in circumstances that could not have been predicted exactly does not mean that planning was incorrect in the first place. But planners prefer to be precise rather than flexible.

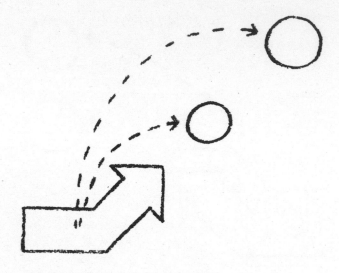

93 SHORT-TERM AND LONG-TERM OBJECTIVES

The drawing suggests that the short-term objective is a step on the way to the long-term objective. In a general sense this is probably always true but it need not be true in a detailed sense. A corporation may get into a certain line of business as a short-term objective simply in order to generate cash-flow, a customer base or a better price-earnings ratio in order to move on to something quite different. There can be an oblique or 'dog-leg' approach in which the short-term objective may not seem to fit with the long-term objective. It is an objective for today and tomorrow and every day as it arrives. Is it a matter of a year, two years, or a five-year plan? Is a short-term objective anything more than the tactics required from moment to moment in order to implement the over-all strategy that is going to lead to the long-term objective? There is no answer to these questions. It all depends on the nature of the business. In general a short-term objective would be eighteen months to three years ahead and a long term objective ten to fifteen years.

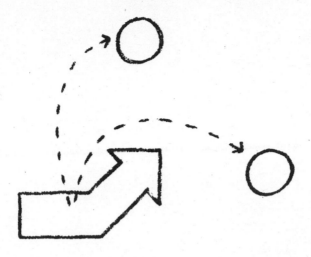

94 CONTRADICTORY OBJECTIVES

Elsewhere in the book I have written about problems that are impossible to solve because the solution requires a basic contradiction. Contradictory objectives are not quite as bad. It is easy enough to set up an objective which really consists of two contradictory objectives: that is to say that to reach one you have to move away from the other (for example, lowering prices on premium goods, designing a family sports car, designing tyres that do not wear out). In a way contradictory objectives become self-defeating because as we move towards one objective we move away from the other. For instance, as we build up an initial market share with a tyre that does not wear out we move away from the long-term profitability because replacements fall sharply. For some people the ambition to be liked and to be successful is a contradictory objective.

95 WRONG FIT

The volume seems about right but the shape is quite wrong. The visual examination of shape is easy but in all other areas the examination of 'shape' is extremely difficult. We use the word 'profile' to indicate that we are trying to look at a shape when we are selecting people, choosing a business to take over, assessing a deal, estimating a risk. A shape is a collection of features. It is difficult enough to find out the features that matter, even more difficult to assess them and almost impossible to see how they fit together. Should you promote a man who is effective and has leadership qualities but is very difficult to work with? Should you accept a package deal that contains many assets but some businesses that are going to provide a hefty cash drain? In a face, a slight shift of the same features can change beauty into oddity. History might have been different if Cleopatra's nose had been longer or Napoleon had been taller. It is often more difficult to assess the 'shape' of the receiving organisation than the shape of what is being received. We might get a good idea of the shape of the man we are promoting but do we really know the 'shape' of the job he is going into?

96 INADEQUATE FIT

Inadequacy has a negative connotation. This can be a danger. There are obviously situations where inadequacy can be a disaster. The hyfil turbine blades of the RB 2–11 aero engine were inadequate to withstand a bird-strike. An inadequate person in a job can lead to a sharp fall in morale or sales. An inadequate price for a product leads to bankruptcy. In other cases, however, inadequacy merely means that we have not got as much as we would have liked. An inadequate meal leaves us feeling hungry. Should we remember the hunger or the enjoyment of the meal whilst it lasted? An inadequate return on capital might mean that we are getting less than we would if the money was at work in the money market, but whereas the development of the business is within our control interest rates are not. Clearly there is a spectrum ranging from 'inadequate' that is clearly wrong to 'inadequate' that is only just short of our greedy expectations. There is a trade-off between cost and perfection. The pragmatist knows it better than the idealist.

97 EXCESS

A sledge-hammer to crack a nut. Are we buying more data-processing than we really need? Do we need highly qualified graduates for all these jobs? Is this fashion label worth the high price? With inadequacy or a wrong fit we have no doubts, but about excess we are ambivalent. If we can afford it, what does the excess matter? If the person is over-qualified for the job we have a bonus. If we do not need all that DP equipment now we may need it in the future. Quite recently many corporations have discovered that they were considerably over-insured and that by re-structuring their insurance and taking over some of the risks their costs could be reduced. This came about because insurance is a good thing and having more of it is better, if you can afford it. Excess is insidious because at the time it seems a bonus but later on it can be an expense that diverts resources from development areas. Zero-based budgeting is a method for looking afresh at all the inbuilt excesses that we have come to take for granted.

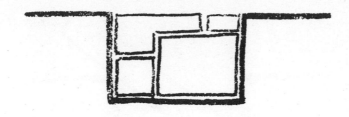

98 COMPLICATED

There are some people who relish complication. They like fitting together intricate Chinese puzzles. They like the complexity of a deal when in the end all the bits fit neatly together. They are, in fact, suspicious of anything simple and easily bored with it. Academics love complication for the sake of complication because it is a highly marketable substitute for ideas. The drawing suggests that a good fit has been achieved. But is this enough? Aesthetics and elegance may have little to do with a business situation but complication signals trouble. Trouble in maintaining the fit, trouble in servicing the fit, both arise from complication. Complicated political formulas work for a while and then fall apart. Complicated things are never robust and things that are not robust require a disproportionate amount of attention. Their failure rate is high.

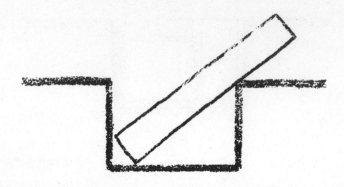

99 PRE-EMPTION

The drawing suggests that the reception area has been pre-empted by a completely inadequate shape. It is worse than inadequate because, unlike the inadequate shape shown earlier, which still allows the remaining space to be filled, this one blocks the space. In an expanding business, like television in its earlier days, senior positions are filled by the young people available at the time. These positions are then pre-empted for a long time as the incumbents have many years to go before retirement. More talented people cannot take charge. When we examine something we tend to examine it within its own context. Does it work well? Does it do what it is supposed to do? Are there any problems? It is much less usual to examine something to see what else could be done with that position, how else the resources could be used. Research departments are filled with projects which seem valuable when each is examined on its own. But many of these worthy projects could be replaced by even better projects that had now become possible because of technical development. School subjects are all worthwhile but the time-table is filled and many of these subjects are pre-empting spaces that could be filled with subjects much more relevant to the modern world.

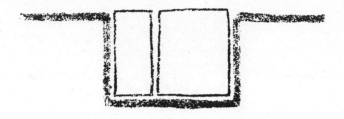

100 COMBINED FIT

As jobs become even more complicated we have to look harder and harder to find a suitable person to fill them. Nowadays a chief executive has to have a strong understanding of finance, he needs to be good at public relations, he must understand technology, he must be able to cope with labour problems and he must (as always) be a good selector of people. There are times when we need to appreciate that a requirement may be filled by two things in which one partner has one set of talents and the other partner another set. The history of successful entrepreneurs very often shows such a tandem approach between the conceptual man and risk taker on the one hand and the solid back-up lawyer (or accountant) on the other. Instead of looking for one thing to satisfy our needs we might try looking for combinations. Needless to say this is much more difficult. Two genuine half-wits do not make a genuine wit and two specialists do not make a generalist; but two tools may do a better job than one multi-purpose tool.

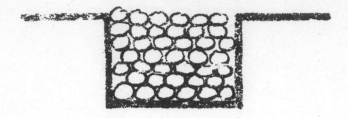

101 STANDARD UNITS

The cavity in the drawing is filled with ball-bearings. Whatever the shape of the cavity it could be adequately filled with ball-bearings. The units are small enough to fill up the space almost as a liquid would fill it. There is nothing specific about the ball-bearings: nothing that makes them more suitable to one situation rather than another. In real-life terms, the equivalent standard units that can be of help in any circumstances are money, time and people. These standard units can 'fit' any situation. The output that results depends on how well structured the situation is to make use of such standard units. The philosophy of the assembly line was to break down the work into simple elements that required no special training. If we are going to use standard units then we need to structure the demand situation in such a way that the required output needs no more than the standard units. On an acquisition level, it means only looking at the assets, market valuation and cashflow rather than at the nature of the business. It may well be that one consequence of increasing complexity will be a return to standard units. Complexity will be shifted from the ingredient to the container.

102 ADAPTIVE RECEPTION

In this drawing the reception 'hole' has changed to accept the contents. In all previous drawings in this section it was a matter of trying to fill a particular hole. In this case it is the hole that is showing the flexibility. In the UK, if a talented person applies for a job he will be turned away if there is no vacancy; in the USA a job is likely to be created to take advantage of that person's talents. It is natural to set out to look for something with a rigid set of requirements: to know precisely what we are looking for. It is not easy to adapt our requirements to something valuable that we come across. It is not easy because, carried to extremes, it would be a dangerous policy which would not be unlike that of a bargain hunting housewife at a January sale who buys things she will never use because the price is right. As always the human mind is uneasy in 'balance' situations. The mind prefers the security of absolutes: 'It is always correct to do this'; 'This should never be done.'

FUTURE FORECASTS

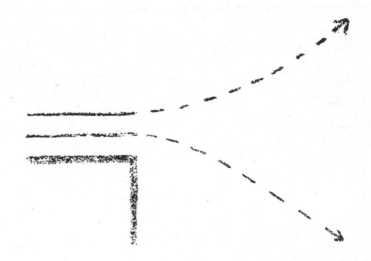

103 WIDE UNCERTAINTY

The present ends at the edge of the cliff in the drawing. Then
we launch into the unknown future. The solid lines of certainty
gave way to the broken lines of uncertainty. The top line (of
the pair) represents the 'best-case' scenario. This is the most
optimistic view of the future. The lower line represents the
worst case. Somewhere between the best case and the worst
case we suppose the actual future to lie. If in our plans we
hope for the best and are prepared for the worst then we should
be ready for anything in between. In the drawing there is so
wide a divergence between the upward curve of the optimist

and the downward curve of the pessimist that most situations are covered. There is a wide degree of uncertainty indicated by the wide splay between best and worst cases. In fact the uncertainty is so wide that it is doubtful if the forecast would be of much value. If a forecast maintains that almost everything is possible, the reader of the forecast is not much better off then he was before – except for one thing. He now knows that there is no scenario more likely than any other. This negative knowledge could be valuable.

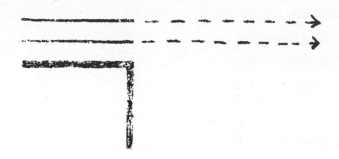

104 EXTRAPOLATION

Here the forecast extends the present trends into the future. Most forecasts work this way because there is no other way to work. If we are not going to guess, there has to be something to work on. The only thing there is to work upon is the present and past. So we take some trends and ignore others. Or we may put different trends together to produce a novel outcome. All these are examples of extrapolation. Even if we had a method which did not use extrapolation it would not be much use because no one would believe the result. Results are only acceptable if they can be logically related to present-day trends. In this particular drawing the forecaster has assumed that the future is going to be almost the same as the present (at least in the characteristics he is depicting). Although this assumption is very likely to be wrong it is still a usable forecast in the sense that it may be no more wrong than forecasts of change that get it wrong. It could be argued that predicting no change is a more reliable strategy than predicting change and just guessing at what it might be.

105 DEGREES OF GLOOM

Both best and worst cases show a downward trend. The only difference is that the slope of the worst case is rather steeper than the slope of the best. At least we can infer that there is no cause for optimism. We prepare for the worst-case slope and then are agreeably surprised when disaster takes longer to come than expected. There have always been small groups of people who have predicted the end of the world on some seemingly significant date (like the year 2000) and sold their possessions to sit on a mountain top. It is difficult to tell whether they are disappointed or pleased when the expected end seems delayed. It sometimes makes good sense to get into a declining business. Everyone in that business is rushing out and no consultants are advising entry. Disaster may not be as imminent as everyone expects and there may still be fat profits to be made by those with good nerves. The degree or rate of gloom is important even when the fact of it has been accepted.

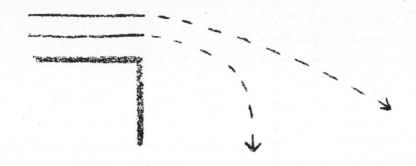

106 ACCELERATING DISASTER

This is rather similar to the preceding forecast except that the worst case curve signifies accelerating disaster. The curve shown suggests a positive feedback that works towards disaster. It is not the curve of air leaving a balloon or a slowly disappearing market but the curve of system-breakdown. So in this case the difference between best-case gloom and worst-case gloom is qualitative not just quantitative. Inflation is different from hyper-inflation. In looking into the future it is always difficult to tell which changes are going to happen within the system as we know it (democracy, capitalism, banks) and which changes are going to alter the system itself. When you are playing a game of Monopoly with someone you may not be able to predict his strategy or the roll of the dice but you can predict that he will stick to the rules of the game. In forecasting the future there is no certainty. The rules themselves may get changed. In general, the complications introduced by having to predict changes both of system and of behaviour are so great that most forecasters assume that the system will not change (except by evolution) and claim that if everything is going to change there is not much point in having a forecast anyway because there will no longer be an organisation to act upon it.

107 STABLE STATES

Both best and worst cases show a decline stabilises as a steady state. The level of the state is considerably below the present level (in output, productivity, profits, standard of living, GDP or whatever). The worst-case steady state is far below the best-case, but the general shape of the future is the same in each case. Such a forecast would not attempt to predict the moment-to-moment changes that have led to the steady state. There may be considerable turmoil and upset before the system re-stabilises. Steady-state forecasts are always based on some assumptions about social system behaviour. There are assumptions about feedback and checks. There are assumptions about the balance of demand and supply. There may even be unjustified assumptions about the rationality of human behaviour. In general, steady states, however bad, are much easier to work with than curves and fluctuations. Of course if the forecaster has merely averaged out considerable fluctuations to give an overall steady state that is less useful than a genuine steady state. There are many businesses (like commodity trading and stockbroking) that depend on fluctuations.

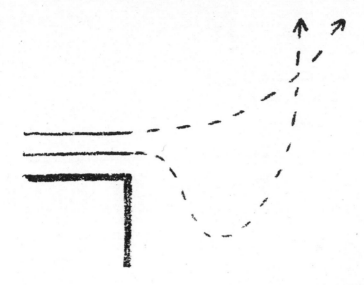

108 OPTIMISM

In this drawing there is the curious suggestion that the worst-case curve actually crosses the best-case curve to give a better result. This paradox is easily explained. The best-case curve shows an accelerating optimism: things get better and better. The worst-case curve shows an early disaster. From the ashes of this disaster in a phoenix-like manner there arises a new system or a new concept that is much more successful than the old one. For example from the relative disaster in automobile manufacturing might arise a new concept of the car that is amazingly successful. This is a somewhat unusual view, for prophets of disaster usually see it just as a disaster, not as a necessary stepping stone to something better. It is rather difficult to communicate the emotion of gloom and at the same time radiate joy. The phenomenon is, however, quite common in ordinary business. Over-capacity leads to a fall in prices and bankruptcies. This is followed by a shake-out in which the weaker competitors are killed off. There is then a wonderful opportunity for those who have survived, because the field is clear and for some time newcomers are chary of entering it.

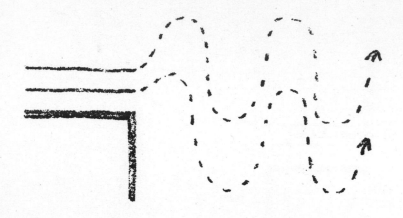

109 BUMPY RIDE

This forecast suggests that the future will consist of business cycles just like the present and the past. As before, on the upward part of the curve people will predict eternal boom and on the downward part they will predict disaster claiming that the situation has changed permanently. The worst-case forecast also shows curves only here the peaks are not so high and the troughs are much deeper. The interesting question is whether business is more at risk from short-term fluctuations or long-term trends. Businesses are becoming increasingly brittle. Partly this is the result of increasing size and competition but it is also the result of a financial philosophy which cannot countenance waste and so removes cushions. The frequency of the cycles and the nerve of bankers will determine whether short-term cycles or long-term trends matter most. If the cycles matter most, then we may well be wasting our time with long-range forecasting.

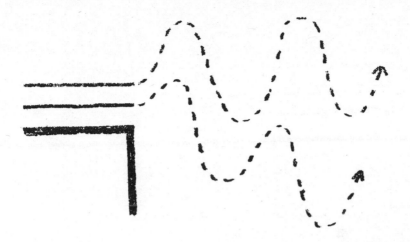

110 BASE-LINE DRIFT

Again the forecast shows cycles, but this time the worst-case curve shows that each successive peak is at a lower level than the one before and each successive trough is deeper. The fluctuations are superimposed on a baseline that is drifting steadily downwards. In general this is the sort of forecast that is currently being made about Western industry. Recessions will be succeeded by boom but competitive pressures will erode margins, wage demands and the cost of social expectations will curb profits, institutional investors will play safe elsewhere – and so on. Does the downward drift matter? Should one invest more in order to be ahead of competitors? Should one invest less because the returns are declining? Should one get out of the business altogether in order to enter another business which is probably doing the same? Unless the slope of the baseline drift is very steep the decline has few practical consequences except to sharpen competitive pressures. Most long-term drifts are accepted as part of the dynamic nature of business.

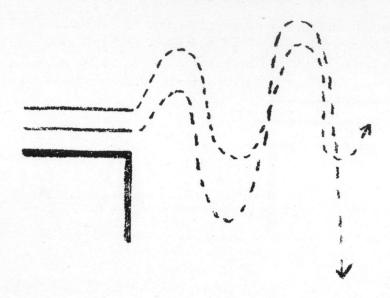

111 WILDER FLUCTUATIONS

The worst-case curve shows fluctuations that get larger and larger. Indeed, at one point the peak of a worst-case fluctuation actually exceeds that of the best case. Business fluctuations have been getting larger and larger. For this there are many explanations. Increased speed of communication means that people can act much more quickly and can make trends into self-fulfilling prophecies. Replacement markets for many manufactured goods mean that consumers can postpone purchases more easily. Instead of buying a car every second year the motorist can make his purchase every third year so creating a considerable fall in sales. There are few cushions in the system. Both panic and greed act as fast as they can via telephone or email. The speed of others creates the real fear of being left behind. Add to this huge amounts of institutional funds, Eurodollars and oil money and volatility seems only natural. The drawing suggests that there might come a time when the system does not recover at the bottom of its dive but continues heading downwards to collapse. It seems logical to suppose that wilder and wilder swings must in the end get out of control. But those whose very livelihood depends on such fluctuations are unlikely to recommend the damping of the system.

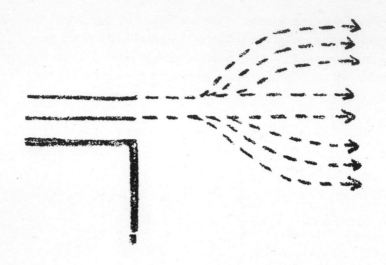

112 MULTIPLE SCENARIOS

Each of the scenarios can be precise and detailed but there are many of them. You take your choice as to which seems most likely to you. The creation of such multiple scenarios is not really a cop-out. It is an acknowledgement that there cannot be certainty but that there are only a limited number of possible event-patterns. In practice you look at all the alternatives and examine each in turn to see how it might affect your business. You design your business so that it can live with most of the scenarios and actually profit from many of them. The multiple-scenario forecast is considerably more useful than the broad band of uncertainty which declares that anything might happen between widely separate best and worst cases. The method acknowledges that there are laws of organisation which ensure that trends coalesce into defined patterns. At the same time there is the danger that such multiple scenarios may be no more valid than creative fiction writing. It all depends on the purpose for which we need a scenario. It may be to enrich our imaginings.

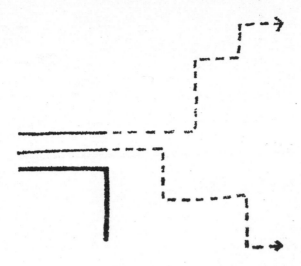

113 DISCONTINUITY

All the forecast curves shown so far have been more or less smooth. The drawing shown here suggests sharp, step-like changes. These are discontinuities since there is no continuity between the change and what has gone before. There could be a sudden breakthrough in nuclear fusion or the cost equation of photo-electric energy. There could be a war or there could be the epidemic spread of a new ideology. There is no honest way in which a forecaster can legitimately be expected to insert discontinuities, because by definition they are unpredictable. He can imagine a variety of possible discontinuities, as I have done here, and he may use each of these to construct an alternative scenario; but this by no means exhausts the possible discontinuities, most of which cannot even be conceived at the moment. Perhaps we shall return to slave cultures like the Greeks of Athena. If we cannot predict or cope with major discontinuities should we bother about them? The answer is that we can gamble on their occurrence and their nature by so arranging matters that we might profit from them. What we cannot do is to rely on their happening.

PLANNING

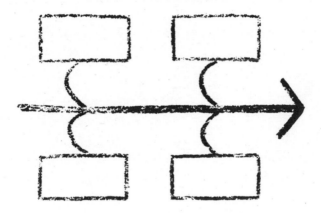

114 PLANNING

There are two ways of walking along a rocky beach. You can carefully plan each step, or you can run along much faster, adjusting your balance with the next step you take. Instead of planning to have a stable foothold at each step, you recover from a bad step with the next one you take. In the same way, it is possible to move forward in a free-wheeling way, making adjustments as required and recovering from mistakes. Without intricate and detailed planning the construction of a building would be slow, wasteful and chaotic. Planning is essential to make sure that resources are used most effectively. There is no point in having to wait weeks for the concrete scaffolders, nor is there any point in having the site cluttered with pipes that are only to be needed later. The drawing suggests how resources are linked together to give the over-all thrust of the plan. A plan consists of time, resources and indicated action but the whole is much greater than the sum of the parts. It is the degree of integration and the thrust of the plan that matter. A plan must have dynamism otherwise it is not a plan but a map of a storeroom. A plan is meant to make things happen – not just describe what is happening anyway.

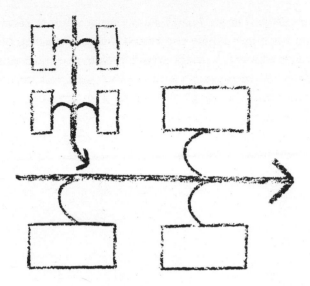

115 SUB-PLAN

The drawing suggests how a sub-plan feeds into the main-stream of the over-all plan. There may be sub-plans for different departments or sections of a department. On the building site the electricians may have their own sub-plan. How do sub-plans arise? There seem to be three possible ways. The first way is for each department to make its own plans without much regard to the others. In the end these separate plans are cobbled together by a central planning department and adjusted to make them compatible. Even if there is a great deal of consultation between departments at each stage, the plan is likely to have a patchwork effect, especially if timing is crucial. This type of planning may be motivating but is not very effective. The second method is for central planning to make the master plan and then to hand over the outlines of a sub-plan to the departments who fill in the details of their own sub-plan. The third method is for central planning to work out every detail of the plan and ask the departments to follow the plan exactly. The difficulty here is that central planning may know very little about the actual way of working of the different departments, so a theoretically superior plan may be impracticable. As usual, it is a trade-off between perfection and practicality with the second method being preferred.

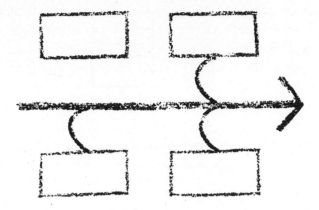

116 INCOMPLETE PLAN

A plan that is incomplete is just not a plan. The drawing suggests how a sector of resources has been ignored and is not linked in to the over-all plan. Instead of laying down detailed action at each step a plan may allow for flexibility or contingencies. For example, if the price of metal rises too high there may be a switch to plastic. These areas of flexibility need to be defined very carefully and the possible options spelled out as far as possible, for in a tightly knit plan a sudden deviation at one point can set off a chain reaction of confusion throughout the plan. In the case of an incomplete plan it is very difficult to fit in later what has been overlooked in the beginning. Naturally planners are reluctant to designate an area for mistakes and oversights, because to anticipate these means that the plan is not as perfect as all planners assume their plans to be.

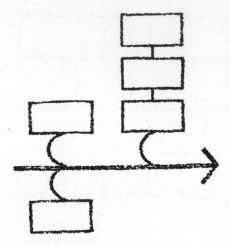

117 PATCHY

The drawing suggests how a great deal of attention has been paid to one area but other areas have been ignored. This very often happens in planning because some departments makes them vague in comparison. For example an R & D department can specify the resources it needs and even the direction of its work. Target dates and cut-off dates and review procedures can all be specified, but the time taken to solve a problem or make a break-through cannot be predicted. In planning, as elsewhere, there is a tendency to deal thoroughly with those areas that seem amenable to our procedures and to deal superficially with the others. We may not be able to plan the unplannable but we have to accomodate it in our plans.

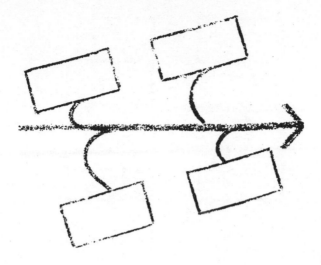

118 UNNATURAL

Since a plan is a process of deliberate choice and decision, it would seem that the output could never be called unnatural; for in a sense the whole process is unnatural (if contrasted with unplanned evolution). Yet some plans are natural and others unnatural. In a way this is no different from the aesthetics of a design. There are 'natural' designs that seem to flow and there are others that are awkward and 'unnatural'. The drawing suggests an unnatural plan in which the designed thrust of the plan does not follow the alignment of the resources. A plan of this sort can always be worked out and imposed on a situation, but it is unlikely to work smoothly. An unnatural plan runs counter to the laws of organisation, the alignment of resources, the culture of the organisation and the idiom of the business. This is not to suggest that plans should be left to evolve in a natural way. Just as a sculptor deliberately creates something but follows the flow of the wood so a planner deliberately creates his plan but follows the flow of the organisation.

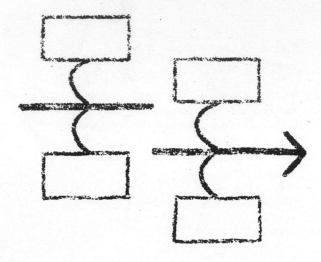

119 DISLOCATION

The drawing suggests a plan that has been abruptly dislocated. The spine of the plan has been broken. It may be that there has been a failure of performance in a key area. It may be that outside circumstances like an OPEC price rise have caused the dislocation. Should plans, like earthquake-proof buildings, be designed to resist dislocations? Plans should contain alternatives, fall-back positions and contingency arrangements but there is a limit to flexibility. Plans can be designed to 'fail safe' in the sense that failure returns the organisation to its base position rather than propels it to disaster. In practice, however, plans will fail and will get dislocated. How long do we try to patch up a failing plan? How soon do we abandon it and put together a new plan? Some countries operate five-year plans but there is nothing sacred about this length of time. A plan may be designed as a five-year plan and may need changing after one year. There is no contradiction here. A boat that sets out for a destination may have to renavigate on the way or may even have to change destination.

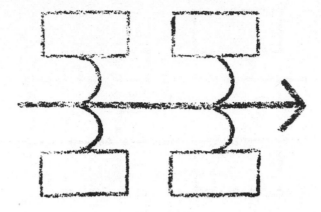

120 FRICTION

Comparison of this drawing with the other ones in this planning section will reveal that the linking curves are facing the other way. In the other drawings the linking curves flow into the main spine of the plan. In this drawing the curves flow against the thrust of the plan. This is intended to symbolise friction. Clausewitz, the great German philosopher of war, used the term 'friction' to cover all the hassles and difficulty that could interfere with the smooth running of a plan. This is the sense in which 'friction' is used here. Friction does not prevent motion. But it does mean that much more effort is needed. It means that energy is required to overcome the friction as well as to move forward. It means that any slackening of energy will lead to a rapid slowdown. Friction embraces resistance or resentment on the part of key people who have to implement the plan. Friction includes cumbersome procedures and also lack of feedback information. Friction includes legal delays and matters like the SEC in the USA and the Competition and Markets Authority in the UK. Friction may involve the training of new executives. In short it covers all those matters that slow down the smooth flow of the plan.

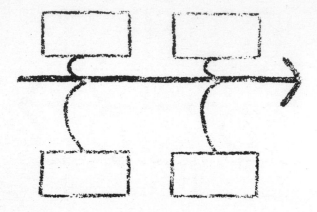

121 UNBALANCED

Plans often have a bias in one direction or another. There are production-oriented companies and marketing-oriented companies. A plan may have a bias towards the financial structure or towards technological development. The bias means that the favoured area is given preference. The path of development for that area is the optimal path and it is preserved in the plan. The other areas have to be made to fit around it. Since it is unlikely that all preferred paths would have an exact alignment there have to be changes of alignment. The favoured area becomes the reference to which the others have to be aligned. There is no real reason why a plan should be 'fair', 'unbiased' or 'democratic'. The heads of the different divisions might feel that it should be so but that is only a claim of ego and emotion. What is important, however, is that the bias should be conscious and deliberate and a matter of corporate policy. It should not be introduced by the planner on his own initative or under pressure from one department head.

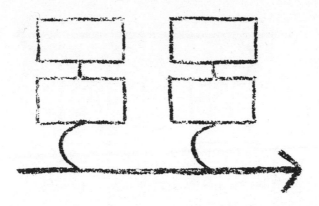

122 TOP-DOWN

A top-down plan is one which is derived directly from strategies and objectives. It is based less on where the corporation is at than on where it wants to get. It is a plan for change and movement. It is a plan for growth and development. The concepts expressed in the plan may not yet exist in the organisation. The plan is the action plan for a great deal of thinking that has been going on. The plan is thinking-based. That is not to say that it is out of touch with reality but that planning for the future requires thinking. The relationship between strategy and planning is very important here because too many organisations do not make the distinction. A strategy should never be allowed to evolve as a by-product of the efforts of the planning department. Strategy is totally different from planning. In fact it is dangerous to allow strategy and planning to be handled in the same place. This is because strategy can so easily be influenced by the needs, idiom and comfort of planning. For example, planning likes forecasts and figures and this would tie strategy to areas that could provide these. Planning is a service for implementing strategy not creating it.

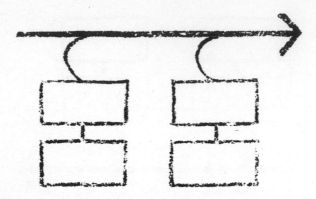

123 BOTTOM-UP

Here the planning is resource-based. It is based on the resources, assets and habits of the organisation. The plan is designed to make the best use of these resources and to protect that best use into the future. Such a plan is based more on where the company is at than on where the company is going. It is a maintenance plan rather than a change plan. This does not mean that it is simply an exercise in resource management. It means that the starting point for the plan is not a strategic concept of the future but an assessment of the resources of the present. Clearly there is a considerable overlap between top-down and bottom-up plans, but the fundamental distinction needs making. The preferred type of plan will depend on the nature of the organisation, the state of the market and the style of the chief executive. A retail organisation might choose a bottom-up plan, so might an airline. A bank would probably choose a bottom-up plan but should be choosing a top-down one.

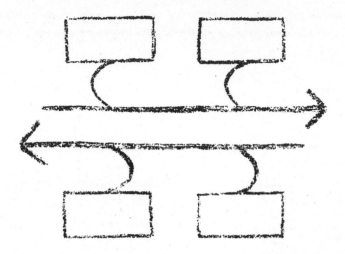

124 CONFLICTING PLANS

The drawing is explicit: there are two plans moving in exactly opposite directions. It is not likely that an organisation would embrace two plans that were pulling against each other. Yet it can happen that the momentum of the previous plan (or previous chief executive) is still pulling in one direction whilst the new plan (or chief executive) wants to go in the other direction. An old plan may no longer be operating officially but it may still be operating unofficially. Heads of different divisions may informally set their own plan which is not moving in the same direction as the handed-down plan to which they pay lip service. At this point I am not writing about open conflict, mutiny, factions or friction, but about a quiet pulling in a different direction. On the surface all is well; but the steps taken are danced to a different tune. It is not inconceivable that a dedicated Marxist might be more interested in the long-term plan for the collapse of capitalism than in the survival of the corporation with which he works. That is an extreme case but a marketing man may subtly resist the plan to move from premium pricing to commodity pricing, or he may sabotage the plan to squeeze more profit out of old products rather than spend money on new ones.

INFORMATION

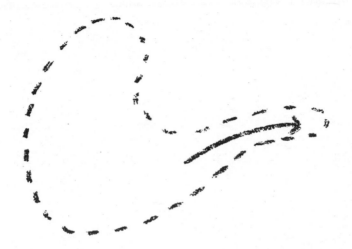

125 THRUST

The broken line represents the information 'field' available to the thinker. The arrow suggests the direction of his effort. In this particular case the information field is being extended in one particular direction: there is an information 'thrust' in that direction. Focused effort and determination can yield a surprising amount of information but the motivation has to be high. We are all so bombarded with information that it requires a lot of willpower to set out to find more information. Information-retrieval is often irritating and slow. Action-oriented people prefer to leave information-seeking to others. Yet even these others (researchers) have to be given a direction and that direction can only come from some pre-existing knowledge in the field. Many successful businesses have been founded on the single item of information that no one is carrying out a particular service or producing a particular product. The innovation element may be very low. Businesses founded on information of this sort are more likely to be successful than those founded on innovation of a more spectacular sort.

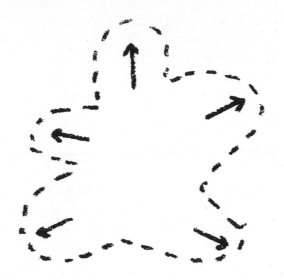

126 GENERAL EXPLORATION

The arrows point in different directions as the field of information is enlarged at all parts of its boundary. The search for general information is more difficult than the search for specific information because all directions are relevant. It is an old piece of advice that if you want to work in an area (insurance, real estate or food) you should spend some time working in that area. It is good advice for there is no substitute for the sort of general information that can be gathered in this way. No amount of brilliance can make up for knowledge of the idiom of the field. If you have not time to acquire such general knowledge in a field then you hire someone who has. But you do not have to hire the smart guy at the top, for his thinking is likely to be atypical anyway. You hire a conventional thinker in that field. From him you get the idiom, conventions and know-how. From this basis you produce your own bright ideas.

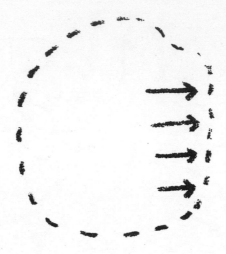

127 BROAD FRONT

Military commanders sometimes push a salient forward but at other times they advance on a broad front. In the drawing an attempt is being made to enlarge the information field on a broad front: it is between the general exploration and the focused thrust. This is the sort of exploration that is done, or should be done, in a take-over situation. It is not enough to look at the company's accounts: the nature of the market, the stance of competitors, likely technological changes have all to be considered. A sound company in a faltering market may not be worth the price. Buying promise has a certain value but there is nothing exclusive about promise. Broad-front exploration is expensive and tedious so we tend to look for some key factor that will simplify the task. If it is an assessment situation we look for someone else's judgement. We trust other people's judgements more than our own for the simple reason that we know what our judgements are based upon. Information is a raw material like any other and buying it is a sensible thing to do. The fact that you might have been able to get it yourself is only relevant if you cannot afford to buy it.

128 LINKING-UP

A large amount of our thinking and information-exploration is concerned with linking things together. We come across isolated pieces of information and set out to link them up. Are the clues part of a trend? What is the over-all picture? What extra significance is added when different items are put together? Hindsight is very good at telling us that we should have noticed trends much earlier than we did because all the signs were available. To link things up we have to act on the information rather than wait for the information to act on us. Significance has to be 'squeezed' out of isolated items. Significance is by no means obvious. Why something is not done may be as significant as why something has been done. Two people can read the same magazine article and one of them will get far more information out of it than the other. Indeed, one of them may get more information out of it than the author realised he was putting into it.

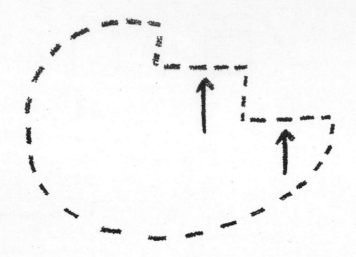

129 FINDING SUPPORT

We have an idea and we want to know if it will work. We have an idea and we want to convince someone else of its value. To do both these we have to find support for the idea. In a few limited cases we can actually try things out in the laboratory or with an engineering model. In all other cases we have to find support in the literature, in what other people have done or in our own experience. History is the only test bed for new ideas that cannot be tested. Of course we choose the evidence that supports our idea and ignore as irrelevant that which does not. Even for scientists there comes a point in the gathering of evidence when conviction takes over and thereafter selects the evidence. Fortunately there is a surprising repetitiveness about human nature: a good deal that has worked in one field is quite likely to work in another field. Something which is dull at first sight is likely to remain dull. Something which is liked by the first person you show it to is likely to appeal to many more people. All this can be formalised in market research. Even better is the possibility of testing things out.

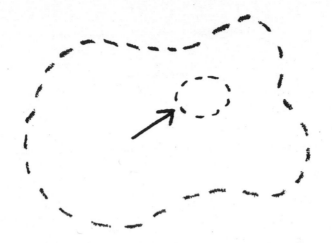

130 CHALLENGE

We tend to challenge other people's information but very rarely our own. It is not that we are afraid to do so but simply that the occasion never really arises. We rarely sit down to challenge some assumption we have always used. We rarely challenge a conclusion we have derived from experience. We rarely challenge our habitual way of doing something. We know that if we started to challenge everything we should end up like the centipede that became paralysed through analysis of the movement of its many legs. Killing off old information or myths is extremely difficult. We do not have, and could not have, a graveyard for old ideas. They have to die through neglect or through being supplanted by a better one. We cannot kill off an old idea in order to develop a better one. The best we can do is to establish a habit of 'challenge' since this allows the old idea to continue but at the same time attaches some doubt and dissatisfaction to it.

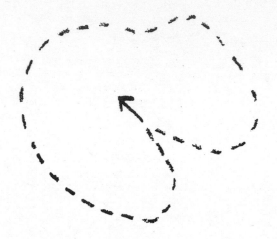

131 DISBELIEF

In the drawing the arrow is seen to be pulling inwards the boundary of the information field. This symbolises 'disbelief', for when
we refuse to believe something we are, in a sense, removing that
thing from our information field. Life is based on beliefs, expectations and assumptions. Everything we do is geared to a belief.
We expect planes to take off on time. We expect people to pay
their debts. We expect products that sell to go on selling. Much
of this belief is soundly based in experience but part of it is based
on wishful thinking. We want to believe something and so get
to believe it. Religion tends to be based on the need of people to
believe in something more important than their own trivial lives.
There is a difference between a 'wish' and 'wishful thinking'.
Wishes provide us with motivation and strategy, for without the
greed of a wish we would never get started. Wishful thinking
creates a fantasy world in which we are to act and inasmuch as
that world is false our actions will be ineffective. The ideal is to be
honest in appraisal and imaginative in desire. We do not have to
destroy all beliefs for some of them – even though false – sustain
useful action. The myths of marketing are an example.

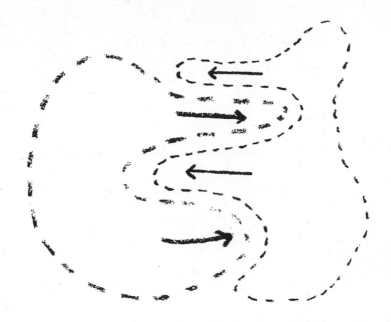

132 EXCHANGE

The drawing shows two interchanging information fields that look like mating amoebas. I have come across very, very few good listeners. Most people use what someone else is saying only as a springboard for what they are going to say. They interrupt because they are unwilling to let pass a remark from which an intricate leap can be performed. Listening means harvesting what is being offered. It means reading between the uttered lines. It means asking promoting questions and also repeating what seems to have been said in order to ask for clarification. At the end of any interchange each party should be able to ask the questions: 'What did I tell him and what did he tell me?' If the answer to that question cannot be verbalised succinctly then the meeting must have served some purpose other than the interchange of information fields (it may for example have had a social value or a 'credit' assessment value).

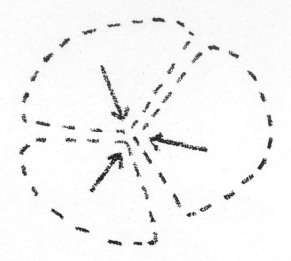

133 COME TOGETHER

The drawing suggests how separate information fields can combine together to form a large field. The separate fields may have been supplied by different people or they may all be in separate parts of the mind of the same person. Maps were created by different explorers who each brought in their own small bit. Spies feed their small pieces of information to the centre where the whole picture is gradually built up. In Japanese industry, decisions are made through a process of information combination. Each person present puts in his piece of information. In time a picture emerges and in time that picture will get into a plan for decisions and action. This is rather different from the Western dialectic habit in which one party will put forward his idea and back it up with supporting information. Another party will attack that idea and use information to further that attack. We use evidence as a weapon in an argument, the Japanese use it as an element in a construction. Evidence can sometimes be contradictory. It is then a matter of teasing out the contradiction, not of dismissing one or other item.

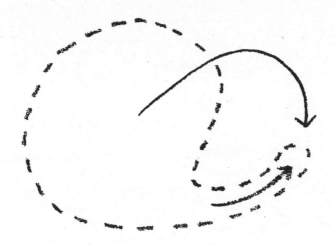

134 PUTTING A QUESTION

The arrow that leaps out of the information field is the question. It arises in the field but moves out of the field to create a destination. An attempt is then made to reach that destination (provide the answer) by extending the information field in that direction. A question is a device for focusing attention. Sometimes it focuses attention on what is known and sometimes on what is not yet known. Asking questions to which we know the answer is a useful exercise because it formalises in answer form what we may have only held vaguely before: 'Why are we doing this?' 'What do we hope to achieve?' 'What is holding us up?' With regard to things we do not know it is more difficult. We can define the unknown in broad terms – 'What would increase our margins here?' – and this is really defining a search area. In essence a question tells us the answer with which we would be satisfied: if our thinking can get us to this point we can stop that line of thinking. As with problem solving, the difficulty with asking the right questions is that we cannot do so unless we already know the answer. But we can get into the habit – and many people do – of asking a number of standard questions that usefully focus attention.

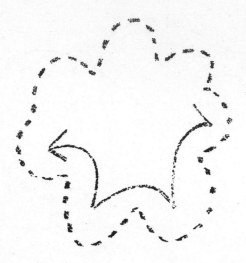

135 DETAIL

There are artists who paint in every detail and there are other artists (like Turner) who convey a mood with undefined washes of colour. Does detail build up to a whole or is detail obtained by microscoping the whole? For thinking purposes there is a useful level of detail with which to work. Above that level it is a matter of broad generalities which do not lead anywhere. Below that level it is a matter of getting bogged down. Good thinkers automatically work at this level, but it is not at all easy to define. Detail does matter because concepts which are excellent in their general sweep can founder on a small matter of detail. Detailed costing can make the difference between an excellent idea and a ruinous one. Movie films always run over budget because the artistic temperament is impatient with detail. To be permanently enmeshed in detail is not to see the wood for the trees. To eschew detail is to float in the clouds above the wood. It is a matter of having to move in and out of detail as part of the general operation of thinking. But detail remains everyone's business.

136 CONSOLIDATION

The arrows in the drawing are moving back from the boundary of the information field to the centre. The field is not being extended any further. Instead there is an attempt to consolidate what is already known. Consolidation is a pleasurable process: 'What does all this add up to?' 'What do we really know?' 'Acting on the information we now have, what would we do?' The mind prefers to work on something tangible than to explore the unknown. With consolidation we are working on the tangible information that is available. Even an uncertainty is tangible: 'What we know for certain is that this point is uncertain.' With consolidation a conclusion of some sort is required. There may be insufficient information, in which case the conclusion is exactly that. One of the more useful thinking exercises is to set yourself, or a group, a time limit at the end of which a conclusion of some sort must be reached. The more specific the conclusion the better. A conclusion does not have to include all the available information: the conclusion may coalesce out of only part of it.

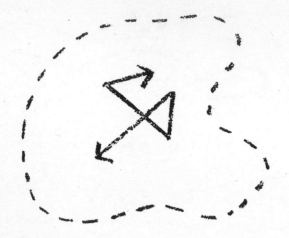

137 CONFUSION

People do not like thinking. At the bottom of this dislike is one main factor: confusion. If there were no confusion, thinking would be highly pleasurable, and much more effective. To avoid confusion we need some sort of structure which allows us to focus on one thing at a time. This is as much to keep other things from crowding in as it is to ensure that we pay attention to all that matters. The thinking programme which I developed (the CoRT programme), which is now the most widely used in the world for teaching thinking, is designed to avoid confusion through the use of specific attention tools. It is now used not only in thousands of schools but also in industry at different levels. If we did not programme computers correctly, they would also get very confused. We take care to avoid this by designing appropriate software. We do not take as much trouble with the mind even though its task is rather more difficult.

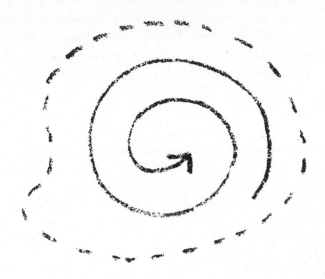

138 SURVEY

In the drawing the smooth spiral scans and surveys the information field. There is an inventory check of knowledge. The mind does not really forget. Under hypnosis it is possible to get a subject to remember in great detail an event that happened years ago and which he thinks he has forgotten. Forgetting is a problem of access. If we do not review our knowledge from time to time it becomes lost to us and we find ourselves thinking within a shrinking field. In Australia the boundary riders would periodically tour around the perimeter of the station in order to check the fences. We also need to do that with our information fields, in terms both of checking the boundary and also of surveying the field. What has changed since we last looked at it? What are the new trends and developments? What is our mechanism for keeping up to date? Are there ideas which were not right for the time but which could be revived and used now? What are the know-how assets of our business?

The more formal the stock-taking procedure, the more effective it is likely to be. It may be that there is now enough information available to answer questions that were asked a long time ago but never answered.

COMMUNICATION

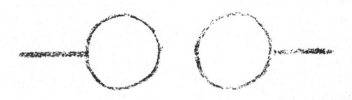

139 NO COMMUNICATION

The two parties are facing each other but there is no overlap between their perceptual 'bubbles'. Each party has a view of the world that is uninfluenced by the other. The environment is continually communicating with us because, through perception, we read the information that it provides. That the environment is not animate enough to want to communicate with us is irrelevant. Communication and the wish to communicate are not closely related. The strongest wish may not effect communication and, conversely, communication can occur when there is every intention of preventing it (as in a bridge tournament). With intended communication, the communicator wants to be that part of the environment to which the receiver is paying attention and also to design what is attended to – in order to produce some effect. The fascinating psychology of interest and attention have not yet been worked out but they are probably no different for communication than for perception in a broader sense. The person offering the communication is, of course, just as much part of the message as the words that are uttered. In McLuhan's words the medium is (part of) the message.

140 COMMUNICATION

The perceptual 'bubbles' overlap. If the overlap were to be complete we would have perfect communication: both parties would have identical perceptions and whatever happened in one bubble would happen in the other. Communication is not a matter of trying to 'put something' into the other person's perception but of arranging for that perception to, temporarily, coincide with one's own. Two people looking at exactly the same thing may have quite different perceptions depending on experience, background and interest. An artist, an art historian and a tourist may all be looking at the same painting but their perceptions would be different. Communication is not achieved by putting something that means one thing to us in front of someone else and hoping that it means the same thing to that other person. The physical means of communication (words, sounds or pictures) only act as triggers. We need to have an idea of what perceptions we are triggering.

141 SELLING

Selling is one stage further than communication. The drawing shows that the perceptual bubbles do indeed overlap. In addition the 'directions' of action are also aligned. This symbolises that the motivation of the receiver is now following the wishes of the communicator. A salesman may communicate perfectly well with a customer but fail to make a sale. Another salesman may communicate imperfectly but succeed in making a sale because one of the triggers used was sufficient to motivate the purchase. The communication needed for selling may be rather different from that needed for instructing. Instructions should be unambiguous, but in selling an ambiguous trigger may be used (not in the sense of deceit) because the salesman knows that different listeners will react in different ways. The salesman tries to shape the perceptual bubble. Presenting a product at its true value to a consumer who does not know about the product requires more than objective information because the consumer may not know how that information relates to his or her needs. The problem is to determine how far this shaped perception can go before it becomes deceit or manipulation. A sick man who values a games console more than a bottle of medicine that will cure him needs to be made aware of the values involved.

142 DIFFERENT LANGUAGES

Communication requires that both parties have similar languages of perception. If the receiver's language is known to be totally different, then the communicator must know how to switch into that language. This obviously applies when the word 'language' is used in its direct sense, but it equally applies when it is used symbolically for perceptions and values. In Germany there are thousands of Turkish 'guest workers'. Attempts are made to teach them German but in practice it is easier to teach the factory foreman enough Turkish to communicate with them. Too often in communication we try to teach the other person our language and concepts and then communicate in this language. We do this because we fear that the other language may not contain the sophisticated concepts we may need in the communication. Trying to teach a concept and use it for communication at the same time is an impossible task. The moral is obvious: always communicate in the other person's language. Yet when demagogues do this successfully they are castigated for it.

143 BARRIER

The drawing suggests a physical barrier to communication so that as the two parties approach they slide past each other. Perceptual barriers act in the same way. They take the form of a context-concept which prevents the overlap of perceptions. The simplest example is a strong 'we' and 'they' concept. Whatever is said falls on one or other side of the barrier. No matter how logical or even how emotional the communication may be, the barrier prevents any unifying of perceptions. Trying to remove the barrier at the time of communication is probably a waste of effort. It is probably best to acknowledge the barrier and so seek to make it into part of the perceptual bubble. Thus a salesman who is meeting sales resistance will acknowledge that he is a salesman and that his motivation is to try to sell the life insurance policy. The barrier is now visible to both sides and can be referred to: 'I would not waste my time selling a policy that was no good because the effort required would be too great – I have a living to make. It is much easier to sell good products.' Age and youth barriers and sex barriers are similar. In all cases it is not a matter of tearing them down (at least not at the time of the communication) but of making them part of the communication.

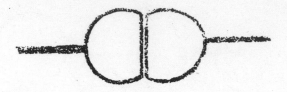

144 PSEUDO-COMMUNICATION

At first sight there does seem to be communication – but there is no overlap of perceptual bubbles. Each side has maintained its own perceptual bubble but these have been made compatible so they fit together as a whole. During the Second World War the capitalist allies worked together with Communist Russia without either side altering its views and without much real communication. There are times when a 'modus vivendi' is a good substitute for communication. The limits and boundaries of the relationship are defined in a Confucian manner, and neither side seeks to make communication the basis for cooperation. The method is probably too little used because communication has an aura of truth about it and our cultural habit is to seek out truth rather than design workable falsehoods.

145 POLARISATION

Polarisation is one of the most natural habits of mind. It arises directly from the pattern-making nature of mind, as I described in my book *The Mechanism of Mind*. It is not just perversity. It may indeed be exaggerated by our traditional dialectic habits of clash and argument, as I have suggested elsewhere in this book, but it does not arise from them. In order to create distinct patterns the mind has to separate things sharply one from the other, just as a driver seeks to separate the road from its borders even in dim light. In all polarisations there is the obvious practical purpose of judgement. The driver needs to know where to drive. The polarising thinker needs to know what he is to agree with and what he must attack. Compromise deprives a thinker of the emotional base that all objective thinking requires. The most emotional thinkers are those who use emotion to drive logic. Paradoxically there is a conversion phenomenon in which a person who is violently polarised on one side may, very suddenly, switch to the other side. It happens in religion and it happens in politics. In fact polarisation is less of a barrier than the barriers described earlier.

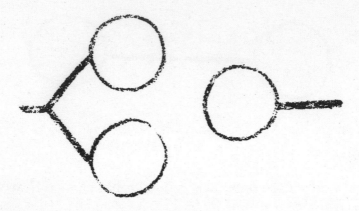

146 AMBIGUITY

Just as confusion is the enemy of thinking, so ambiguity is the enemy of communication. If you ever have to write the rules for a game you will be amazed how rules which seem absolutely clear to you can be interpreted – quite justifiably – in a totally different way by highly intelligent people. Often in communication it may be necessary to spell out not only what is to be done but also what is not to be done. That seems superfluous and even confusing, but unless some paths of possible interpretation are quite deliberately blocked they will be taken. When I designed the L-game it seemed obvious from the rules I had written that the pieces could be picked up and placed anywhere on the board. Most people (used to other games) thought the pieces could only be slid from one position to another. In communication it is so easy to forget that we are dealing with the other person's world and not our own.

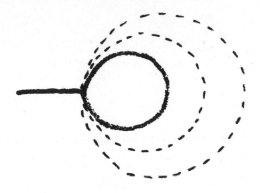

147 FIELD OF COMMUNICATION

What is the field of communication? Is it enough just to give orders and instructions, or is the field of communication wider? Communication within a family involves the context and hierarchy of the family. Communication amongst friends includes a much broader field than what is being communicated at that moment. Within a corporation there may be a sense of team spirit or there may be a corporate culture which becomes part of the communication at any moment. Even apart from these there may be the broad communication area of one human being communicating with another. The opposite style is to assume that the communication should be limited to exactly what there is to be communicated and that all else risks blurring the communication. Should negotiating executives discuss the political scene or the latest art exhibition before getting down to business? Intuition suggests that communication should first be on a personal level and then on a business level because context is so important in communication, but much depends on personal style. Perhaps communication should be at the broadest possible level if that is done well; if not, it should be only at that level which can be done well.

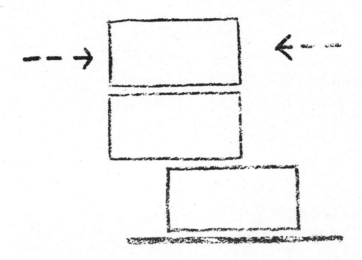

148 STABILITY

The pile of three blocks shown in the drawing would be stable if pushed at from the direction of one of the arrows and very unstable if pushed at from the other direction. The pile has a lot in common with most organisations which are stable when under pressure from one direction but can collapse when under pressure from another direction. The risk of collapse is a risk inherent in any business. It is usually offered as a justification for the rewards that sometimes are to be found. The risk of something collapsing is one type of risk and is similar to the risk of a ship going down, an aircraft crashing or the price of gold plummeting. These disasters are an expected part of the system, although strenuous efforts are made to reduce the frequency of the occurrences. In the block arrangement, there might be a twenty-five per cent chance of collapse if pressures on the pile were to be distributed on all four sides. This degree of risk would be unacceptably high for most business purposes and yet the risk of failure of a new product is very much higher.

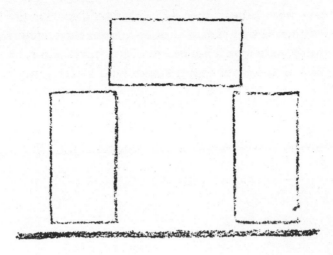

149 VULNERABILITY

The structure shown in the drawing is stable but at the same time it is vulnerable. A shake of the table on which it was standing would bring the pile down in exactly the same way that an earthquake shakes houses down. The structure would have been much more stable if the two supporting pillars had been placed closer together. For the sake of the argument we must assume that the space covered by the arch is proportional to the benefits, so that there has been some purpose in making the arch as broad as possible. So there is a trade-off between benefits and risk: a narrow arch would be more stable, the widest possible arch is the least stable. Outside of danger- ous sports the only purpose behind the taking of risks is the hope of benefit. We accept that a high risk should have a high reward even though this is not always the case in the market place. What is strange is that we often accept the opposite: that large benefits naturally carry with them large risks. There is no logical reason why this should be so. It is true that an obvious field with high benefits and low risk would quickly get over-crowded, but if we generate a new concept there is no reason why the rewards should not be great and the risks low. To think otherwise is to confuse moral justice with business reality.

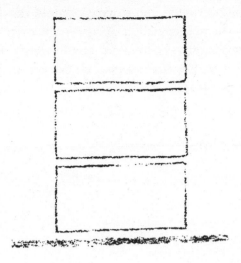

150 BANKERS' RISK

Banks are not designed to take risks. There is no reason why they should. They are money channels that take a fee for the channelling service. For their lending they can select the areas with very little risk. It is only the desire to expand or competitive pressure which drives banks to lend to customers who are not one hundred per cent secure. In countries where banks are the major source of funds for new businesses a dilemma is created. The banks are expected to take up an investment stance which is not their true role. In other countries (notably Germany and Japan) banks have traditionally been investors at least in major industries. Banks prefer to lend short-term because their borrowing (at least from depositors) is short-term and changes in interest rates could lock them into long-term loans that were uneconomical. Lending to the government is more or less risk-free (in stable countries) and there is no reason why investors, or banks, should seek out risks. Greed and the expectation of proper rewards are the only real justification for risk-taking. If banks choose not to be tempted in this way then an appeal to their civic duty is misplaced. A government guarantee of risky loans to new ventures makes more sense. An alternative would be the prospect of untaxed returns for private investors.

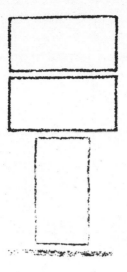

151 INVESTORS' RISK

This structure is less stable than the one shown for 'bankers' risk'. At the same time it is higher. Assuming height to be a benefit the investor is prepared to take a risk in order to get a higher reward. On this basis it makes more sense for an investor to invest in promise than in reality. Once reality has set in the rewards are known. Promise remains open-ended. The investor who invests in promise – as so many US investors do in new-technology companies – has two possible sources of reward. He can sell out his holding at a profit to new investors or he can sit back and await the dividends on the investment. The former policy makes more sense since it is still promise that is being sold on. Today the major source of investment is institutional funds (insurance companies, pension funds, mutual funds) and the strategy for a salaried portfolio manager who controls large sums must be fundamentally different from that of the private investor. For one thing, receiving bodies must be large enough to absorb big amounts at a time.

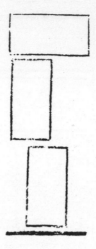

152 SPECULATORS' RISK

The speculator knows that he is taking risky decisions. The investor hopes that he is not. The banker tries to make sure he is not. The drawing suggests a first investment that is very risky for the speculator. So the next investment is used as a hedge to restore balance. The speculator lives dangerously and on his wits. He takes the risks others might not be willing to take. In a way he acts as a risk channel. Later, if the situation matures, the speculator sells on to those who will now accept the reduced risk. The true speculator acts first and adjusts later. On the whole speculation is frowned upon because it sometimes drives prices up in a monopolistic fashion (through the cornering of some market) and because it creates volatility; yet where the speculator is a skilled trader in risks he is part of the system. In a way, a skilled speculator is not unlike a skilled insurance underwriter who accepts risks, prices them, passes them on and hedges them.

153 BROADWAY RISK

The drawing is rather misleading because the three separate pillars should really be very thin and very tall. They should be tall because the benefits are potentially large, and thin because they are unstable. For the sake of graphic unity they are the same size as the blocks used elsewhere in this section. The main point is the separateness and independence of the enterprises. An investor in a Broadway production knows full well that four out of five investments will certainly be lost. The fifth, however, will make enough money to cover the losses and show a profit. This type of risk is rather different from the others described because the Broadway investor knows that the odds are definitely against him on every investment. There is a similarity to the investment in new products (for a food company) for the odds are against success each time. Venture capital falls somewhere between investment risk and Broadway risk. Broadway risk is only ever justified by the huge rewards that come from a success. For this reason, investments of this type only make sense if the success of a successful outcome is in a traditional field where the rewards are known. Broadway risk does not apply in an untested field.

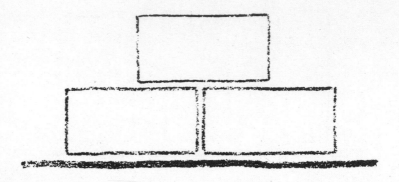

154 INSURANCE RISK

Insurers are supposed to insure risks but not to take them. The drawing shows an arrangement of blocks that is very stable on its broad base. It is the breadth of the base that is significant for the obvious key concept in insurance is the spread of the risk. This spreading effect means that insurance risk is often confused with Broadway risk. A corporation that says, 'Let us spread the risk by not putting all our eggs in one basket' is using neither type of risk effectively. The cost of the failure of one product is not spread in an insurance fashion by having the other products around. Ten bad products are just as likely to fail as one bad product – there is no protection in numbers. If each of the products had a chance of great profitability then there would be true Broadway risk, but that sort of expectation for a single product is unrealistic. The philosophy is the incorrect one of a marksman who feels that, if he shoots enough bullets at a target, one of them will hit it, and that the aim of none of them needs be very precise. It is a lottery philosophy, and lottery risk is something different from both insurance and Broadway risk.

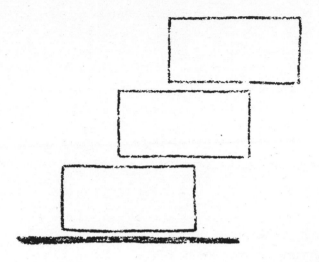

155 INEVITABLE

If more blocks are added to the pile in the drawing in the same manner as those already there, there must come a moment when the whole pile will tip over. Ultimate catastrophe is inevitable. The question is when it will happen. There are those who believe that a major earthquake along the San Andreas fault is inevitable at some time, but meanwhile people live in California and thrive and make money. The 'time risk' illustrated in the drawing is interesting because of the inevitability of failure: the risk is shifted to the estimation of the length of time that might elapse before that failure. Currency speculators operate on this time risk; so do stock buyers when the market is rising or falling sharply: 'How long before the turn?' Pharmaceutical companies with products that are market leaders know that the situation cannot last forever: new products, expiry of patents, generic competition are all inevitable – sometime.

GROUP DECISIONS

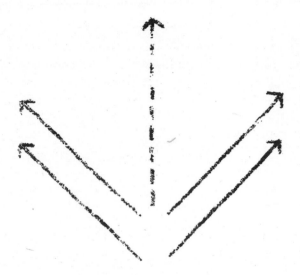

156 COMPROMISE

No one really gets what he or she wants. A midway path is chosen between the diverging aspirations of the two factions. It seems 'fair' to both parties only because it is not obviously unfair to either of them. It is rather like the resultant of mechanical forces pulling in different directions. It is the path a load would follow if it was pulled by the opposing factions in the drawing. The outcome satisfies egos and may prevent trouble, but there is no reason whatsoever why the compromise solution should actually fit the problem. Either of the two opposing views might have worked well, but the compromise is an artefact related to social considerations, not to the problem. Imagine that two doctors are arguing about the treatment of a patient. In fact both treatments would work even if one were to be marginally better. To stop the argument they decide on a compromise: the patient gets half of one treatment and half of the other. The patient gets drug doses that are too low and drugs that are incompatible. This caricature scenario has as much logic as most compromise situations. A compromise might work when each side has a shopping list of independent desires and the two shopping lists are combined. Where a system solution is required, a compromise solves nothing.

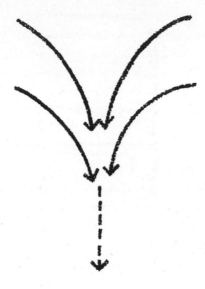

157 CONSENSUS

Gradually all the parties come around to the same view. Their interests and motivations are aligned. Everyone gets what he or she now wants. The final direction of outcome may well be different from the intentions of the participants at the start of the meeting but time and care have been applied to help the participants to arrive at the most effective consensus. It can be seen that consensus of this sort is very different from compromise or voting. The decision is not taken until all are in agreement. It is up to each participant to feel his way towards the consensus outcome. It is not imposed by anyone. It is not a victory of one side over the other. Some members of the group may arrive at the consensus view ahead of the others but even then it is not a matter of persuading the others. The situation continues to be discussed objectively without positions being taken. Those points that have been agreed upon are noted and repeated. In time the consensus view is seen to have emerged. There is no sudden voting. If there is no consensus view for a detailed approach, a general one will do.

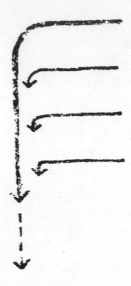

158 LEADERSHIP

The leader is seen to emerge in the drawing and to carry the others with him. They follow willingly. It is not a matter of bludgeoning and bullying them. The leader has taken the initiative. Perhaps he knows more about the field. He presents the case. He supports his case. He smooths away difficulties. He exerts charm and charisma. The others follow like sheep – grateful to be lead with vigour in a specific direction. Perhaps it is the habitual leader of the group or perhaps the leader has arisen for that meeting on that topic. Perhaps the leader has dominated the meeting from the start. Perhaps he has just waited to see what was emerging and then stepped in quickly to take the initiative and carry forward the proposal which he has sensed is about to emerge. There are many different styles of leadership. If the leader is so effective, is the group really necessary? Would the same result not have been obtained without the group? It might have been, but the leader may have needed the audience in order to develop an acceptable idea. The leader may also do a lot of listening but have the qualities, lacking in the others, of putting what he hears into an initiative.

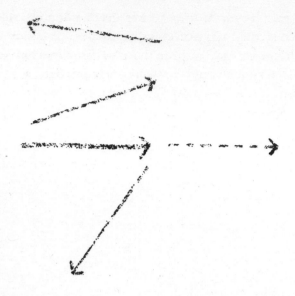

159 POWER

The person with the real power moves straight ahead and decides what should be done. There is no compromise. There is no consensus. There is not even an attempt at leadership. The power person powers ahead conscious of his or her power. It does not even matter what other people are thinking. They are irrelevant except as witnesses of the power and to carry joint responsibility for what has been decided without their help. They may choose to jump on the bandwagon and agree with the decision that will be made anyway or they may choose to cosset disagreements. It does not really matter. The power person may have real power. For example it might be his private company. Or the power person may be a power broker who has arranged his support before the meeting and knows that he can call on it if his authority is challenged. There are some advantages to the system. The person who makes the decision has the power to carry it through. The proposal does fit the situation – which is more than can be said for the compromise approach. The process is very much quicker than the consensus approach. It is difficult to see, however, that it has any advantage over the leadership approach.

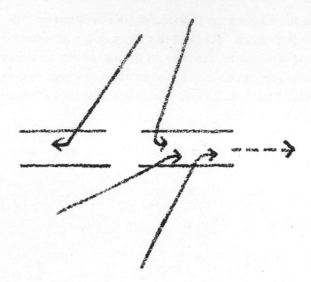

160 VOTING

A motion is put forward. This is represented by the channel in the drawing. Votes are taken. The motion is a sort of compromise which may not truly reflect the views of anyone or even an adequate solution to the problem. The voters align themselves along the artificial channel. There is a majority and the proposal is carried. The participants are not upset because they accept the democratic procedure. But in terms of an effective solution the voting method has little to recommend it. A vote can be forced at any time so there is little effort to build up a better and better solution, as in the consensus method. Those who vote on the losing side are as surely excluded as they are in the power approach. Votes can be used as bargaining counters for future needs. As with the compromise approach the voting approach is designed to soothe the egos of those involved and not to solve the problem. There is no reason at all why the solution chosen by the majority has to be the best one. Indeed, there is a case for supposing that in complicated matters it is likely to be the worst one. Where it is a matter of public feeling then the voting system has a place – as a sort of representative jury. For problem-solving, strategy formulation or appraisal there is little logic to the voting approach.

NEW VENTURE INVESTMENT

161 STEADY AND PREDICTABLE

The drawing suggests a depression or hole that has to be filled. It could be a roadmaker who has to fill a depression in order to continue with the road. The benefits from the completion of the road are great but in order for these benefits to be enjoyed the roadmaker has to invest effort in filling the hole. The drawing suggests that a number of balls are available for this and they are just pushed into the hole one after the other until it is filled and a surface can be laid on top of it. The investment analogy is quite straightforward. The shape of the hole is the investment profile. The extent of the hole represents time. The depth of the hole at any moment represents the money that has to be put in at that moment. The curve is not cumulative: the depth at each point indicates the money that has to be put in at that point. The drawing shown here indicates a nice steady investment with no surprises. It could represent an investment in an R & D department. There is a predictable ongoing cost and at the end there are benefits from each line of investigation. It could also represent a problem-solving type of investment.

162 FRONT-END INVESTMENT

The profile of the hole suggests a typical front-end investment where a considerable amount of cash is required at the beginning and then the drain on resources gets progressively less. It could be a matter of setting up a new plant, opening a new market, launching a new product or turning around a failing company that has been acquired. Initial investments of this type are relatively easy to plan because they are based on actual estimates. There may be snags and complications but, provided there is no great delay, the cost depends on decision: the money that it is intended to spend. It is only later that the effect of this spending becomes apparent and more money may have to be spent to reach an effect that is desired. In the drawing shown this is not the case. It is an ideal scenario, for after the initial heavy cost the spending gets less and less before full profitability is reached. When the plant came on stream the initial sales would start reducing the net outflow of funds which is why the maintenance cost of the operation is not shown as a straight line.

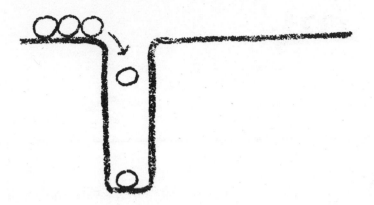

163 RAVINE

The drawing shows a ravine type of investment situation. The opposite bank – which stands for success – seems very near but between where we stand and the opposite bank there is a ravine which is going to absorb a great deal of money. A distillery that wanted to launch a new brand of whisky would face this situation. The launch costs would be huge. There would be no way of doing it gradually or on the cheap. There are many markets where the cost of entry is very large. Buying a taxi-licence in New York or buying a seat on the stock exchange in many countries would be examples of this type of investment. In these particular cases the ultimate cost is known, but in other areas (such as the whisky launch) even an expensive promotional campaign may not be successful. In some cases the ravine could well be shown as virtually bottomless. Critical-mass investment situations are also of this type. A communication system is of no value to the users unless there is a critical mass of users and these have to be bought.

164 HIGH TECHNOLOGY

The drawing suggests the type of investment situation that is often to be found in high-technology investment. At first the investment required seems finite and a goal can be set. This goal is about to be reached when it is discovered that a great deal more investment is required. Things have not worked out as expected, there has been a snag, the line of development has come to a dead end, the promising drug is not safe enough for people and so on. More money is put in, for otherwise the initial investment would have been wasted. Then the same thing happens again – and again and again. To some extent the technology people are to blame for being too optimistic but they realised that if they spelled out the true uncertainty (even if they knew it) there would have been no investment at all. In the end the project is abandoned or has become so expensive that it can never be profitable. The Concorde cost over £1.2 billion in tranches that became necessary exactly in this manner. In the end it does work, but the development costs can never be recovered. Latecomers into the field benefit from all this initial work – at no cost.

165 DECEPTIVE

The investment seems small, for the far bank (in the drawing) seems quite near. But then it turns out not to be a bank but a ridge and a further amount of investment is needed. It is a sort of mirage effect. The investment required to get a small share of a market may not be very large (in some markets) but a great deal more investment is then required to increase this market share to the point where it is large enough to support the operation. The drawing is not meant to suggest the development of unexpected problems like hitting an underground spring when digging the foundations of a new hotel. The total investment need is there from the beginning but it is split into two phases and in our thinking it is only too easy to look only at the first phase because this almost returns the organisation to profitability, and to ignore the second phase which may be essential. We tend to feel that we can always cut off after the first phase if money runs out but in fact we cannot because the whole thing is a single investment. A market share that is unprofitable does not signify a successful investment.

166 HIDDEN COSTS

Here the investment seems simple at first. The hole in the drawing is shallow and the far bank is near. But as we approach the far bank the hole seems to take more and more of the balls. There is a sort of secret cave under the far bank which must be filled before a firm base can be established. The drawing illustrates a situation where heavy hidden costs arise just when everyone is happy that the project is nearing completion. Once again these hidden costs have been part of the investment-need right from the beginning – it is just that they have not been looked at closely enough. A production-oriented company may forget to make proper allowance for marketing costs. A company doing business overseas may not have made proper allowances for the high cost of inducing people to work overseas. The need to set up an expensive servicing network may not have been realised.

167 CUT-OFF

The costs seem to be controlled but suddenly there becomes a demand for more and more money. Should that be supplied or should the project be terminated? That uncomfortable question has faced many investors. Is there a bottomless pit as suggested in the drawing or just a further depression that can be filled with a little more investment? This is not unlike the high-technology investment profile except that it is generalised to situations where the expected risks of high technology are absent. A developer trying to buy up a site in a city comes across an owner who charges a ridiculously high price. Is it worth paying the price or abandoning the project? The traditional problem is that abandonment in many cases means that the investment to date may have been totally wasted, so there is a motivation to keep going. At the same time there is the realisation that if further money is provided and the project still has to be abandoned at the end then even more money will have been wasted. Various calculations can be made as to the continued profitability of the project, the likelihood of further funds and the possibility of selling what has been done so far, but in the end it is still an open-ended situation depending on the calculation of risk. Should there be time cut-offs, cost cut-offs, achievement targets or what? If these are set up in advance do they make the decision easier?

PRIORITIES

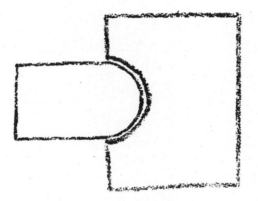

168 TOTAL FIT

The drawing shows a round-headed peg fitting exactly into a socket. What might the priorities be in this situation? Suppose there were just two top priorities: the tip of the peg should make contact with the socket (perhaps for some electrical transmission) and that the peg should be aligned with the socket. If we have a perfect fit between what we want and what we get we do not bother about priorities. The priorities are obviously included in the perfect fit. Priorities only seem useful when we cannot get exactly what we want and we have to settle for second-best. In deciding what we are going to settle for – or in choosing from alternatives – then we might set the priorities and satisfy as many of the most important ones as we can. The question is whether it is worthwhile to check out the priorities even when we seem to have what we want. In general it must be?, because all we have to lose is a little time. On the gain side we might find that a choice which seems very attractive does actually miss out on an important priority. We can get carried away by the sheer attractiveness of the deal or temptation and overlook that priority.

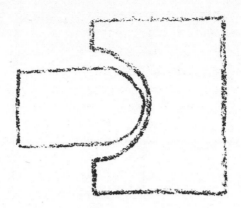

169 SLOPPY

The fit in the drawing is sloppy. We might be inclined to reject the arrangement because it seems unattractive and not what we want. We could reject it at once, just as we might reject a deal which we did not like. If, however, we bother to check the priorities systematically we find that the two top priorities are actually present in the arrangement. The tip of the peg is indeed in contact with the socket and the peg is aligned with it. First appearances can be deceptive because our preferences work on over-all attractiveness not on a check-list of priorities. In selecting people for a job we are inclined to go on general appearance, whether we like the person, whether we would like to have him or her working for us. All these may be part of a general attractiveness but they may be quite separate from the priorities of the job. It is easy to reject someone who is very suitable but whose first appearance is off-putting. It is also possible to accept an attractive and charming person who cannot get the job done.

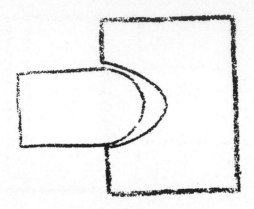

170 ALMOST SUITABLE

Here the fit seems good and the alignment is correct. When we examine it closely we find that the point of the peg is not in contact with the socket so we would have to reject the arrangement. At what point might we be prepared to change our priorities? If we could not buy the material we wanted at a cheap enough price might we drop cheapness from the priority list and buy more expensive material and then pass the price along to the customer? Are priorities absolute or are they things that are important and that we would like to have? A house buyer might reject a particular house because a good kitchen was a top priority and that house had a poor kitchen. The buyer might end up with a much more expensive house which had a better kitchen. Yet he would have spent far less money if he had bought the first house and completely refurnished the kitchen or even changed it to another room. In this case a rigidity of priorities has served the buyer poorly. For a quick screening process of a multitude of alternatives we need rigid priorities but when we can make a more careful examination it is possible to be more flexible.

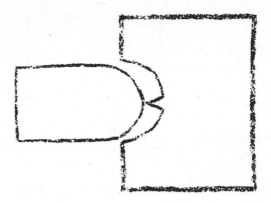

171 MODIFICATION

The drawing shows a modification to the socket. The result looks unstable and inelegant but it greatly increases the chance of the arrangement satisfying one of the two top priorities: that the tip of the peg should make contact with the socket. The small spike in the socket means that the tip of the peg will make contact whether or not there is a good fit. Here we see in action the modification principle which was mentioned earlier. If something does not fit our priorities at first sight is there something we can do by way of modification that will allow the priorities to be met? If we are prepared to look at things in that light then the range of choice becomes much wider. We could in fact formulate a priority which required this possibility of modification. For example in the house-buying case there could have been an alternative priority that the price must be low enough to allow some of the finance available to be spent on modifications. The same argument applies to the choice between employing ready-trained people or being prepared to train them.

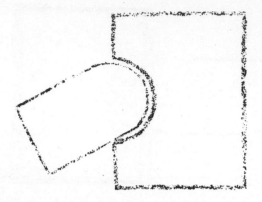

172 TOLERANCE

In the drawing the fit is good, the point of the peg is making contact with the socket but the alignment is poor. Since alignment is a priority the arrangement should be rejected. Just how good does the alignment have to be? Should it be perfect? What is the tolerance? In engineering terms tolerance is the goodness of fit that is demanded. A tolerance of one millimetre means that the measurement has to be within one millimetre of what has been specified. Sometimes priorities can be expressed in absolute terms but at other times absolutes are impossible. If you want to employ an efficient secretary how efficient does she have to be? If you want to build an hotel in an attractive location how attractive does it have to be? If you want to lower the wind resistance on a car body how low do you want to get it? In all these cases the answer would be, 'As good as I can get it.' As so often there is a trade off between practicality and perfection. If there is a relatively free choice of hotel site you go on looking until you find the ideal spot. If few sites are available you settle for something less ideal but still attractive. Where a choice is limited to a few you choose the best of the bunch but ensure that doing so does not ignore other priorities.

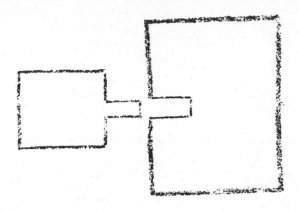

173 DESIGN

The purpose of design is to satisfy priorities. If in the peg and socket arrangement the true priorities were the alignment and the contact then we might re-design the whole thing so that it looked something like the drawing shown here. There would be no need for the round head and the round socket. A more direct fit that was self-aligning could be designed. It would also be more stable. In considering priorities so far we have considered the priorities involved in choice. Equally important are the priorities involved in design. If we set out to design something (a business, a project, a product, a campaign, a job) we need to keep our priorities clearly in mind at each step because after a while the momentum of the design will take over and dictate what comes next. In other words the internal logic of the design may ignore our priorities. In this way a project which would have been profitable evolves into something much more fancy – and more fun – but something which is no longer profitable.

ORGANISATION STRUCTURE

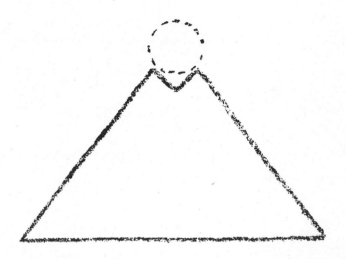

174 PYRAMID

There are many more support staff in the British National Health Service than there are people caring for patients. In the services, it is estimated that for every front-line soldier there are twenty people in support. The pyramid system means that the operating unit is at the sharp end of action and is supported by a very broad base of other services which in turn are supported by others all the way down to the base of the pyramid. There may well be situations where support in depth is vital for the functioning of the front-line unit. There is also the possibility that after a time a support bureaucracy generates its own needs for support quite independently of the front-line units. Any person who is doing a job and is not providing his own support needs supporting. There is a creeping ratchet effect: capacity means something can be done and once it is being done it is expanded or generalised; that in turn means there is need for more support; in turn that support needs supporting, so creating more capacity, and the cycle repeats. With the best will in the world a pyramid structure still tends to expand because a slight change near the apex is multiplied all the way down.

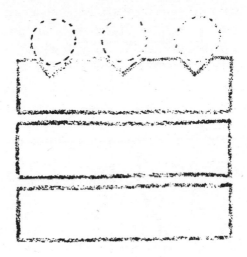

175 LAYERS

In this type of support system the front line units are considered as a layer just like all the other layers. Each layer is an entity unto itself although it interacts and provides services to other layers. In fact the layers are stacked vertically not horizontally as shown in the drawing – the horizontal position was chosen to suggest that the layers were still 'supporting' the front-line units. In a pharmaceutical company there would be a research layer, a communications layer, a production layer, a financial layer and so on. In the end they would all be supporting the front-line sales division. There is quite a difference in attitude between regarding the front-line units as the operating end of the organisation and regarding these units as service units for the rest of the organisation. Production-oriented companies feel that the salespeople have the job of selling what is produced. Market-oriented companies feel that production and research are there to service the sales people.

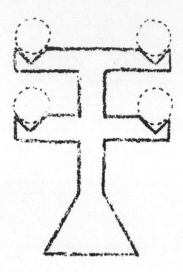

176 TREE

The tree structure illustrated in the drawing is a communication and support system designed to nourish each operating unit providing that unit stays in its place. The units are like the fruit on the tree. Each has its allotted place. The picture is one of classic decentralisation. There is not the freedom of movement there is with the network system but there is far less deadweight of support staff than there is with the pyramid or layer system. It is up to each unit to thrive on its own. From the nourishment of the trunk the unit can draw basic sustenance but nothing beyond that. If things go wrong the centre cannot rescue or support the falling unit – like a dead apple it would simply drop off the tree. The units are expendable and can easily be replaced so long as the tree is healthy. This seems a paradox but it is not: the system is geared to the needs of the operating units but the units are expendable so long as the system remains intact.

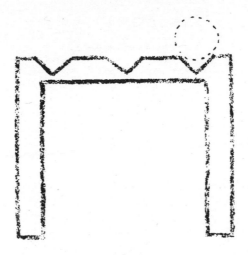

177 NETWORK

The drawing suggests a network type of support system. A number of support centres are spread around and between them is the support network. The operating units have no fixed position but can move about the network from one location to another. That is why some of the positions in the drawing are shown as being unoccupied. At each location the network provides enough support for the front-line unit to operate. In a sense this is a task-force type of organisation, but with the addition of a support network. The system is clearly designed for support of the operating units and there is less danger of a central bureaucratic expansion. The task force can travel quickly because it does not have to carry support material with it. The network also serves as an intelligence system that feeds back local requirements. The franchise system is a different but related type of network in which the operating units are fixed but are linked to the centre by a marketing network. The main disadvantage of the network approach is that areas which are not covered are thereby excluded completely. At the same time it is expensive to cover all areas when the volume of business in some of them is small.

178 GOLF TEE

The operating unit is perched on a golf tee. Just as a golf tee can be pushed into the ground at any point, so the operating unit or front-line unit carries its own support with it. For example a salesman may operate with his own laptop which he plugs in to the telephone system when he wants to obtain or transfer information. There is no support staff as such. There may be central computers but even these may not be required if each salesman (or a group) had a computer and printer at home. In the end support staff act as information switches and this is exactly the sort of function that can be taken over by electronic data processing. The golf tee system is the exact opposite of the pyramid system with its massive support operation. The golf tee structure may not be usable in all situations but it is likely to become more widely used as staff costs increase. In the health area, the old fashioned general practitioner functioned in this way (in contrast to the support structure of a centralised health system).

179 MUTUAL SUPPORT

Here the system is one in which the front-line units support each other. There is no separate support organisation: each unit has the dual function of carrying out the operations and also providing support to other units. Guerilla campaigns and non-established religions tend to operate in this way. An informal network develops but this is different from the fixed network system described earlier. The system is a cooperative one and yet the operating units remain independent. A lightweight structure keeps the units in contact with one another. A unit only continues to operate so long as it is successful. An unsuccessful unit or one that does not contribute its share of mutual support is dropped. Networking of this type is a growing phenomenon in the USA, in particular in the field of out of school education. It is, however, quite easy to pass the point at which an organisation of this sort feels that it can afford a central staff and from that point onwards the central staff becomes essential and the field staff end by servicing its needs and growth.

FAILURE

180 GROWTH

The growing half-span is thrusting forward full of vigour as it symbolises the growth of a business, an idea, a project or an enterprise of any sort. There is direction and there is structure. Growth follows the direction of the arrow – perhaps to meet the other half-span if this were truly a bridge. There are times when the motivations for growth seem clear and times when they are under challenge. There may be a threshold size and till an enterprise reaches that size it is neither profitable nor effective. The field may be vacant and the profits good, growth is not essential but the goodies are there for the picking. There may be economies of scale, and growth may reduce unit cost. Growth may discourage competitors and may discourage others from entering the field. Growth may mean cash flow for new ventures and the ability to make the occasional mistake. Growth may be a matter of achievement for the executives. Growth may be needed to keep the shareholders and stock analysts happy otherwise the share price might decline. Growth may be a matter of momentum: the money comes in and it is better to invest it than pay it out in taxes. Growth may be inevitable or it may be fun. It may also be a mistake.

181 EDGE PROBLEMS

The centre is sound and still vigorous but there are problems at the periphery. The drawing shows a terminal piece that has broken off. Expansion is becoming difficult. Mistakes are being made. New ventures are failing. New products are not giving the return on investment that is the company norm. Perhaps the edge is too far from the centre. Perhaps the managerial talent that was responsible for the steady growth is spread too thin. Perhaps expansion is taking the company into areas for which it has no expertise. Perhaps the centralised structure of the company is no longer suited to the size it has now reached. There may be a need to decentralize and set up semi-autonomous subsidiaries or affiliates. Perhaps it is just a failure of the communication system. Perhaps the decision process is too slow. Perhaps overconfidence has meant the taking of poor risks or a laziness over homework. Edge problems may have a multitude of causes: most of them are structural.

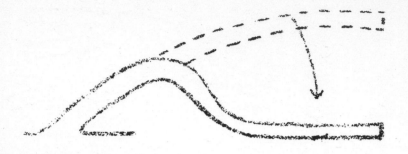

182 SAG

Like a wilting flower the half-span has gently sagged to the ground. There has been no sudden rupture, just a loss of turgor and slow collapse. Dynamism and tautness have disappeared from the enterprise. It has become static and stagnant. Momentum keeps it alive. There are products and there is cash-flow, and for the time being survival can continue. There is a serious loss of morale. It may be the fault of senior management. It may be the accumulation of years of neglect and the milking of cash-cows without thought for the future. The cause is almost certainly internal and not due to market pressures. Perhaps the company is fat and flabby and this weight has caused the sag. Perhaps the chief executive is nearing retirement and has lost interest. Perhaps the company has been taken over by a larger group which is not interested in building it up. A fall in morale tends to be insidious but can be rapidly reversed with definite and positive action. The action has to be more than complaint and exhortation. It needs to be visible action and leadership. A spirit of enterprise may have to be injected into ventures that are justified even if only on this basis.

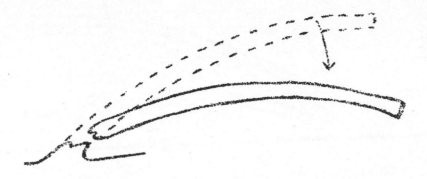

183 SNAP

The base can no longer support the half-span which snaps off.
There is central failure. There is a cash crisis. The banks will
not lend more money and indeed call in their loans. There is
nothing wrong with the periphery which may still be vigorous
and successful but the centre has given way. So taut is modern
business that bankruptcy can happen with surprising swift-
ness. Up to the limit of borrowing there is no problem, but as
soon as that limit is passed there is a crisis sometimes followed
by collapse. The dilemma is that it is difficult to take avoiding
action: if activities are cut back there is no way of retaining
or regaining market position – if activities are increased that
means more spending and more risks. After the usual cost-
trimming exercises have been accomplished the only thing left
to do is to sell off some of the most profitable parts to raise
cash. That lessens the chance of profitability and alarms the
banks that have insisted on these sales. The vicious spiral has
commenced. In fact this is not unlike the collapse of a span, for
a crack at one point concentrates the stress around that point
accelerating the collapse.

184 SPLIT

Part of the half-span has split off and is collapsing but the other half is sound. There often comes a point in the growth of an enterprise when it is clear that some of the activities are profitable and others are a burden. It may be that exports are forging ahead whilst home sales sag – or the other way round. It may be that larger cars are not selling whilst smaller cars are. It may be that the fast food division is doing well but the institutional catering is not. The cause may be a poor product or competitive pressure or the general economic climate. What are the prospects for recovery? What changes can be made? Is it worth killing off the unsuccessful part in order to concentrate resources on the successful side? Are rescues ever worth the effort? Perhaps the unsuccessful divisions can be packaged and sold off to someone who believes they can be made to work. The old adage that eighty per cent of profits come from twenty per cent of the business invites the removal of the inefficient eighty per cent of the business. But what happens after that? Is the same process repeated on what is left – and then again (like one of Zeno's paradoxes)?

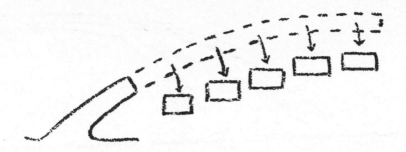

185 DISINTEGRATION

Like a glass shattered by a soprano's voice the span disinte-
grates into small fragments. Everything comes apart. Such a
disaster can only arise from the inherent structure and culture
of the company. There is unlikely to be any external set of circumstances (other than a revolution) that would bring about
a collapse of this type. There has to be a certain brittleness
and poor design to begin with. Surprisingly it can happen
in retail chains when the strategy has gone badly wrong and
trouble occurs on all fronts at the same time. Corporations
are not very good at picking up things that are wrong unless
they are reflected directly in the sales figures. There are rarely
early warning systems for other aspects of the organisation.
As with everything else we rarely design for trouble or failure
because that would threaten our confidence regarding success.
Traditionally sailors thought it unlucky to learn to swim.

186 NEW ROOTS

In mangrove swamps the branches send down new roots which take hold and then support the branch as it moves ever further out. This is suggested in the drawing of the half-span. A new support is seen to descend from the span. The analogy is with parts of an enterprise that are allowed to establish their own base and make their own financial and marketing decisions. It is the conglomerate process in reverse. It is difficult to see why head office should be delighted at the prospect of losing the control they have hitherto exerted and enjoying the cash-flow from the healthy divisions. And yet from every other aspect the process must make sense. Rolls Royce Motors was able to continue as a successful company when the parent company went bankrupt (restructuring had to take place at this point with government help). One of the arguments against decentralisation is that the peripheral units can become complacent and lazy and unwilling to take the risks that the financial resources of the centralised company make possible. This is a genuine problem.

BASIC THINKING

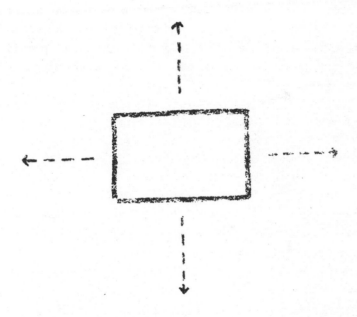

187 EXPLORE

The drawing illustrates exploration in all directions. In our
thinking we follow the perceptual maps of the world that
we build up in our minds. General exploration creates these
maps, extends them and enriches them with details so that
we can follow the bye-ways as well as the high roads. Once
we have good maps our reactions and actions will be appropriate. There is no substitute for information. We gather that
information through reading, asking, listening, consulting

computers and watching both real action and screens of different sorts. In science or engineering we use instruments to amplify our senses. General exploration means more than just looking for what we want. It means being open to new information even when it does not seem immediately relevant. To look only for what we want means that we stay locked within our present knowledge and ideas. General exploration provides the background that enables us to link up otherwise unrelated items. The purpose of exploration is exploration. The value of exploration is as a basis for our thinking. To find our way about we need mental maps: exploration creates those maps.

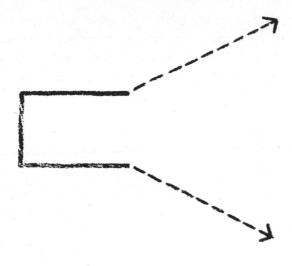

188 SEARCH

Search is more focused than general exploration. There is a direction in which we are looking. This may be a particular segment or sector of the environment or it may be as intensely focused as the search for a particular piece of information. We may set out to search with a tight specification of what we want to find. We know what we want before we start. In the drawing the box is open at the search end and in the search we hope to find something that will fit exactly into that box. A search-light may scan the sky looking for aeroplanes or it may move to that part of the sky where they are expected to be. When searching, we may know where to look or we may have to scan around to find out where to direct our search more intensely. Sometimes we are in a position to make our search easier by setting up filing systems in advance. At other times we search for someone who can then do the searching for us. The main point about a search is that we know what we are looking for and often we know where to look. Knowing where to look can be a danger if it completely stops us from looking elsewhere as well.

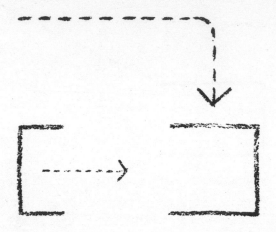

189 POSING A QUESTION

One of the more remarkable, and useful, aspects of language is that it enables us to pose questions. The arrow at the top of the drawing suggests the posing of the question. A question is something that has to be 'fitted'. The second part of the box then moves – as an answer – to fit the question. General exploration is general, search is search in a defined area for something defined, a question is the most specific of all. A question is a way of defining what we do not know. A question places an information target ahead of us. Asking questions is much more important than answering them. The framing of questions is an important skill. In general there are two sorts of questions. In the 'fishing question' we hang out the bait and do not know what sort of answer we will get (for example: 'What media approach could we use here?') In the 'shooting question' we have a specific aim and the answer is usually yes or no (for example: 'Is TV the right medium to reach our focused target group?') We should be in the habit of asking questions of ourselves as much as we ask them of others. A question is an attention-focusing device, especially on things that we do not yet know but know that we do not know.

190 PROJECT

Project is probably the most important activity of all in thinking. We all have to live in the future: the next minute, the next day, the next year, the next decade. Our actions take place in the future. The things we set out to make happen are going to happen in the future. When we drive down a road the road is the future: it is ahead of us. So with projection we run into the future the plans or actions that we have conceived. In our mind we watch them happen in the future. We try and run before our eyes a film strip of the future happening. It is much more than just looking at the ultimate consequences. It is a matter of moment-to-moment projection. An inventor, a scientist or an entrepreneur projects into the future to see the result of his gadget, his experiment or his enterprise. The child who puts one block on top of the other wants to see what happens. Sometimes when we project into the future we have a reasonable expectation, based on experience, of what will happen. At other times there is more uncertainty. All our actions from crossing the road to buying gold involve projections into the future.

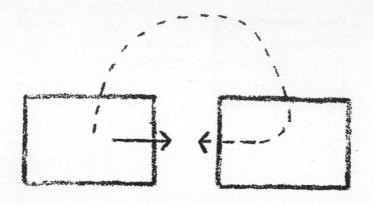

191 OTHER VIEWPOINT

This is the most important 'people skill' in thinking. The drawing suggests how the thinker moves himself into the mind of the other person to see how things look from that viewpoint. Whether it be communication, selling, negotiation, teaching, confrontation, or anything else involving people, the ability to see their point of view is crucial. Seeing that point of view does not mean agreeing with it or even empathising with it: it simply means being able to see what the view is – to look at things from that viewpoint. There is a difference between placing yourself (with your own experience and motivation) in the other person's shoes and trying to see what his view is (with his experience and motivations). This is an important difference. The thinker enters the mind of the other as an observer not as an actor. The most effective people are often those who can see the point of view of others and do not agree with it. That is a sound basis for setting out to communicate, persuade, sell or argue. We also need to see other viewpoints in order to predict the effect of some action. If some change is being made we need to look into the viewpoints of all those who are going to be affected by the change. If we are designing or promoting a product we need to look clearly into the viewpoint of the consumer – and this is not the same as his needs.

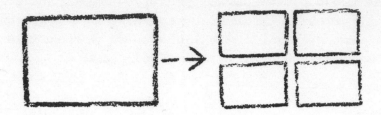

192 ANALYSIS

Analysis is really part of recognition. Thinking can only make use of the patterns we have acquired in the past. When we come across something new we try to recognise it whether it is a person or a disease or an inflection in a chart. If we can recognise it then we know about it (a person), or how to tackle it with a standard solution (a disease), or what the significance may be (an inflection in a chart). But if we cannot recognise something as it stands we try to analyse it into parts that we can recognise. If we succeed then we try to infer the behaviour of the whole from the known behaviour of the parts. When we analyse an event we try to break it down into forces, links and parts. From such an analysis we can pick out causes and action points: we are then in a better position to understand what is happening and to do something about it. Analysis is not absolute. Two people may analyse the same thing in a different way. In some cases, however, the component parts are standard (as in chemistry).

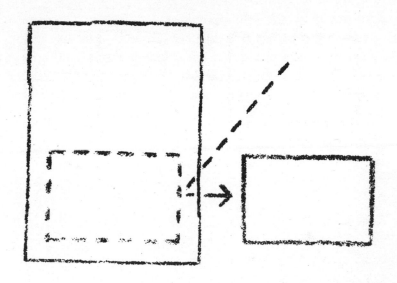

193 EXTRACT

Extract is a form of recognition and a form of analysis but is somewhat different from both. As the drawing suggests, the process of extraction means extracting a significant item from a whole. The difference between a good thinker and an average thinker is often the difference in ability to extract something significant from where it is buried amongst other matters. Extraction is a matter of pattern recognition but it also involves the ability to cut across interfering patterns. It is not like picking a brick out of a brick wall but of creating the shape of a brick in a concrete wall. A caricaturist looks at a face and extracts the significant features so that with a few lines he creates a likeness. A mimic does the same. Most of us tend to see things as wholes or else to analyse them into the obvious parts. The ability to extract is rare precisely because it may have to cut across these obvious parts. It is not search because we do not know precisely what we are looking for. The pattern, as it were, springs out from the background rather like it does with the Ishihara test charts for colour blindness. Of course, our minds have to be sensitised to these patterns. To pick out the important point from amongst the details is a most valuable skill.

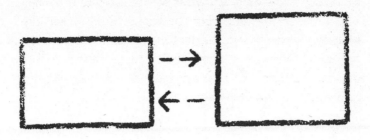

194 COMPARE

Compare is another aid to recognition. We come across something which we have not come across before in exactly the same
form but there is a similarity. We compare what we are seeing
with what we know, to see if there is enough resemblance for us
to treat the new thing in the same way as we would have treated
the known thing. If we can successfully compare a present-day
situation to an historic one then we can use hindsight to tell us
what may happen next. Starting with Aristotle, elaborate clas-
sification systems have been built up to show that things may
belong to the same class (and therefore have common features)
even if their appearance is different. In the biological world we
have the genus for the class and the species for the variations.
In making a comparison we may be looking for points of similarity in order to aid our recognition (and consequent action) or
we may be looking for points of difference. The 'lumpers' like
to put everything together and the 'splitters' like to separate
things by focusing on differences. Many arguments are based
on one side lumping and the other splitting.

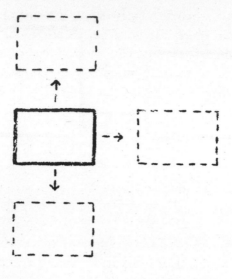

195 ALTERNATIVES

'At this point is there any alternative?' That is a most powerful question. We need alternatives to enrich our choice for decisions. We need alternative plans of action. We need alternative ways of looking at things. We may need alternative explanations or interpretations. We may need to find alternative means to achieve some end. Few people realise just how basic is the need deliberately to look for alternatives. As a pattern making and using system the mind must accept the first acceptable answer. So unless we train ourselves to find alternatives then the better answers that might be hidden behind the first answer are lost to us. It is not a matter of looking for an alternative when the present answer or proposal is unsatisfactory. What is much more important is deliberately to look for alternatives even when the present answer or proposal seems highly satisfactory. That is because this satisfaction may fit our limited expectations or current framework. It is a sort of complacency beyond which we need to go. There is no absolute limit to the number of alternatives that can be generated in a situation, so we can impose a practical limit of three or four or five. If these are easily achieved we go on a bit longer.

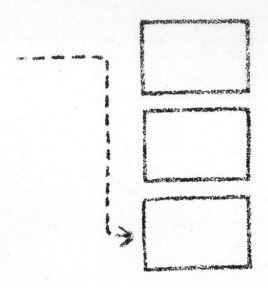

196 SELECT

In the end thinking has to move on into action. Action involves commitment. We may conceive several alternatives but we can only act on one of them. So selection is the important basis for action: in making decisions, in choosing people, in reacting to events. Selection will be based on our priorities, on explicit criteria and fundamentally on our emotional reactions. The purpose of perception is to arrange our choices so that the right one will be made emotionally. After a selection has been made it is a useful exercise to spell out – to oneself as much as to others – why that selection has been made. As suggested elsewhere, one of the problems with selection is giving up the attractive paths that are not being chosen. If selection is difficult then more attention should probably be paid to generating further alternatives which are more attractive or combine features. It is well to keep in mind that the purpose of selection is action: what comes next. We do not choose the best alternative but the one we can best do something about.

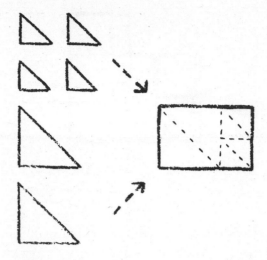

197 SYNTHESIS

Synthesis is part of the thinking involved in making something happen. The carpenter puts together shaped pieces of wood to make a table. The banker puts together different contributions to make a syndicated loan. The poker player puts together a winning hand. The cook puts together the ingredients to make a salad. Synthesis goes beyond mere assembly, for the parts may be integrated with each other to make a functioning whole. Different pieces of information may be synthesised to give a total picture. With synthesis there has to be a desired purpose. Analysis can be done for its own sake (or pure knowledge) in order to see into what parts something can be coherently divided. Apart from playing around with shaped blocks or mathematical functions, synthesis tries to achieve something. The exception might be the synthesis of information which may achieve the same aim as analysis.

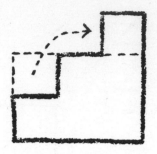

198 DESIGN

Design involves doing something or making something happen. At the end there is something which was not there at the beginning. Something has been created (although it may not be 'creative' in the other sense of the word). Synthesis and design overlap in this matter of bringing something about. But design may involve shaping, trimming, substraction or translocation (as in drawing). It may be a matter of designing jeans, an aero engine or a financial instrument. The idiom or the 'feel' of the material must be known – just as a dress designer needs to know how cloth hangs. The methods of working must be known. Then there is the purpose of the design; aesthetic, communicative, convenient, novel, efficient, etc. The priorities must be met. The constraints have to be obeyed (price, legality, size, etc.). We think of design only as applying to aesthetic matters like furniture or graphic art but it applies to everything. This books has been designed: by me in the first place with my subjects, writing and drawings; then by the print designer. Every business is designed: first as a concept then as an operating system. Design is much more than problem solving. One design may be very much better than another design from which it is only slightly different. A design aims to be effective.

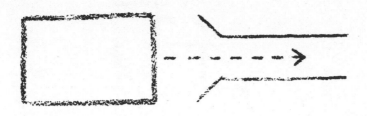

199 PROCESSING

We feed the information into a computer and the computer does the processing for us. We feed the figures into a mathematical formula and the formula then takes over and does the processing for us. We have developed very powerful processing instruments to help our thinking. These will get better and better and we should consider them as part of our thinking. In time data-processing will take over much more of our thinking. For example, the 'optimising' type of design can be taken over by computers. But the perceptual and conceptual part of thinking is likely to remain a task for man. It is up to man to look at the world and through his perceptions and his thinking to convert the world either into a form which can then be processed or into an idea. If we consider the mathematics of combinations we must come to the conclusion that the pattern-making activity of the mind is far better designed for conceptual thinking than any computer. Nevertheless we must delight in computers as our processing slaves and we must promote them rapidly to do more and more thinking – stopping short of allowing ourselves to become slaves to them.

200 PROVOCATION

Provocation is the basic process of lateral thinking which is a much more specific term than creativity for the changing of concept and perceptions. A patterning system like the mind creates patterns which we then continue to use. Most of our thinking is concerned with fitting things into these patterns so that we can act usefully and effectively. But to change patterns and to unlock those 'insight patterns' which are readily available to us (only after we have found them) we need something entirely different. Provocation is the process. With provocation we do not describe something as it is or as it could be. With provocation we look at the 'what if' and 'suppose' and go even beyond these with 'po' the new word I coined elsewhere to allow deliberate provocation (it stands for provocative operation). Poetry is provocative because it goes beyond prose which is descriptive. Provocation creates an unstable idea so that we may move on from it to a new idea. Thought experiments like those used by Einstein are classic examples of provocation.

CONCLUSION

Provocation is a good note on which to end the book, for in a way the book is a provocation. Like all provocations it is meant seriously but not solemnly. I am quite serious about the use of the book as a communication system (as described in the introduction). For the system to work you would need to ensure that your colleagues had a copy – and if that were the case they might even read the book.

For those who might be interested in such peculiarities it can be recorded that this book was written entirely on aeroplanes in the course of a trip to North America: London to New York (British Airways flight 177); New York to Los Angeles (American Airlines flight 3); Los Angeles to Toronto (Air Canada flight 792); Toronto to Edmonton (Air Canada flight 643); Edmonton to London via Toronto (Air Canada flights 126 and 856). The final execution of the drawings and the typing out followed laer. The thinking was done at various times before – and will, no doubt, be re-done by the reader.

Also by Edward de Bono

Parallel Thinking

Western thinking is failing because it was not designed to deal with change

In this provocative masterpiece of creative thinking, Edward de Bono argues for a game-changing new way to think. For thousands of years we have followed the thinking system designed by the Greek philosophers Socrates, Plato and Aristotle, based on analysis and argument. But if we are to flourish in today's rapidly changing world we need to free our minds of these 'boxes' and embrace a more flexible and nimble model.

Parallel Thinking is an invaluable insight into the word of creativity; de Bono unveils unique methods of brainstorming and explains preconceived ideas of what creativity involves and is. This book is not about philosophy; it is about the practical (and parallel) thinking required to get things done in an ever-changing world.

In this extraordinarily prescient book Edward de Bono sets out his method for achieving the ultimate 21st century goal: work-life balance.

Defined in terms of life-space and self-space, de Bono invites the reader to look at their life and measure the gap between these spaces – the smaller the gap, the greater our chances at happiness; but if the life-space is vastly bigger than the self-space, our coping ability is compromised and anxiety is likely.

For anyone concerned with happiness and life-fulfilment this book is essential reading, and is perhaps more resonant with readers now than ever before.

First published in 1967, this remarkable title from one of history's greatest minds remains a must-read in the world of creative thinking.

Based on the belief that an error can lead to the right decision, de Bono guides the reader through a series of problems and puzzles, all designed to help us analyse our personal style of thinking and to consider the potential methods that we never use.

There are three courses, each five days long and each created to focus on a different style of thinking. A true life-changer, this book will have you thinking in way that you never thought were possible.

'THE MASTER OF CREATIVE THINKING'
INDEPENDENT ON SUNDAY

EDWARD
DE BONO

FUTURE
POSITIVE

CHANGE YOUR MIND-SET
FOR A POSITIVE FUTURE

Why are we more prone to be negative? And how can we become more positive, both as individuals and as a society? We need to develop new concepts: some brand new and some slightly different. We have to make a deliberate and positive effort to secure a positive future; we must harness the focused power of human thinking unleashed from its pettiness.

Since Future Positive was first published in 1979, our belief in the power of positive thinking has only deepened.

De Bono was on to something in 1979: the future is positive – if we want it to be.